Reflecte

To Bill
all good wishes
Brenda Bullock.

Reflected Glory

by

Brenda Bullock

**Brewin
Books**

First published August 1999
by Brewin Books, Studley, Warwickshire

ISBN 1 85858 145 1

A British Library Cataloguing in Publication Data
Catalogue record for this book is available from
The British Library.

Typeset in Baskerville and
made and printed in Great Britain
by SupaPrint (Redditch) Ltd., Redditch, Worcestershire.

Foreword

Just as with her first two books, "A Pocket with a Hole" and "Over the Wall", Brenda Bullock goes back to her early life for the inspiration for "Reflected Glory"; to the 1950s, the golden age of football, when, as a girl football fan, in the days when not many females followed the game, she watched the great players of the era: Matthews, Finney, Wright, Lofthouse, while all the time nursing a determination to play for England alongside the heroes she worshipped from the terraces every Saturday afternoon.

The story starts in the 1950s, with a football-mad, poor, working-class kid, totally dedicated to supporting the Wolves, through the great age when they won the League title three times and Wolves and Villa won the F.A. Cup and Birmingham reached the final.

Then came the Sixties, and the mad scramble to raise more and more money to pay players' wages, just at the time when hooliganism was keeping many spectators away from the grounds. By the Eighties the game had been brought to its knees, with Wolves coming within three minutes of ceasing to exist at all. Then came disaster after disaster: Bradford, Hillsborough, Heysal; which brought the future of the game itself into question, and the innocent days of the '50s, with its deep bond between fans, players and clubs, seemed a world away.

This is a personal story, part comic, part serious. It's the story of one football fan, a woman, and is illustrated by some of the wealth of memorabilia that a lifetime of watching football has created. It's the story of a fan who had once found a sense of belonging in supporting a football team, and of the game which had once offered to poverty-stricken kids like her, hope, a sense of pride, and no small ration of "Reflected Glory".

Dedication

To Matt, Graham, James & Ian (who do not support the Wolves) and Jim (who does).

Acknowledgements

Thanks to the following, for permission to use copyright material:

Aerofilms Ltd., Borehamwood
Birmingham City Football Club
Matthew Bullock
Leicester City Football Club
Leyton Orient Football Club
Wembley Stadium Ltd.
Wolverhampton Wanderers Football Club

Although every effort has been made to trace the owners of the copyright of every illustration in the book, the age of some of the pictures has made this impossible in some cases. However, we should be glad to hear from anyone who owns the copyright of any of the illustrations that have not been acknowledged.

By the same author:

A Pocket With a Hole   Brewin Books

Over The Wall   Brewin Books

Contents

CHAPTER 1

The Beginning

If celebrity football fans are to be believed, their passion for the game was kindled very young – in the cradle, no less – and they graduated straight from romper suits into replica Chelsea strips and a life-long season ticket to Stamford Bridge. Not so in my case: my first sport was boxing, arguably a skill of more use on the post-war Council housing estate in Birmingham where we lived, than a penchant for close ball control or regular goal scoring. I had taken up boxing by accident, really. When he was twelve, my brother suffered a little mild bullying at the Boys' Brigade, and my father, who had been a more than useful boxer in his youth, decreed that he must learn what my dad called euphemistically, 'the art of self defence', which, of course, really meant 'how to render your opponent satisfyingly senseless'. Which is where I came into it. I was unanimously elected as sparring partner, against whom my brother would practise all his new-found boxing skills. Thus began my brief and inglorious career as a prizefighter.

Now, at that time I was eight years old, a terribly skinny little kid, and with arms that resembled something out of a Meccano set. Boxing gloves were attached to the end of my skeletal arms, and I flailed about ineffectually, in a vain attempt to connect with any part of my opponent's anatomy, my waving arms looking like demented lollipops. All the while, my brother danced round me, a superior smile playing about his lips, landing punches virtually at will on my puny frame, while I waved my windmill arms, striking the air and almost overbalancing with the effort. One day, however, sheer desperation led me to lash out with even more wild abandon, which, by some glorious accident, landed a blow flush on his nose, sending blood syphoning deliciously in all directions. Horrified, and rendered faint by the sight of so much of his precious life-blood so carelessly spilled about the yard and up the wall of the coal-house, he decided to relinquish the gloves for ever, which allowed me to retire gracefully from the ring, technically undefeated, and to follow the greats of the sport from a safe distance.

My father was a friend of Randolph Turpin in the glorious days when he wrested the World Middleweight Championship from the great Sugar Ray Robinson on that memorable night in London in 1951. Okay, so he lost it again a couple of months later in the rematch in New York, but for a short while at least we basked in his reflected glory. We listened to his fights on the radio, sitting in the kitchen in the half-light, hanging on to every word of the commentator and feeling every punch landed. As I sat in the flickering firelight, hearing the buzz of the crowd, the barely suppressed excitement of the commentator, it all seemed so glamorous to me: a primeval struggle for supremacy, with protagonists called mysteriously and menacingly, "The Brown Bomber", or "The ghost with a Hammer in his hand", or Roland La Starza, a name more reminiscent of Hollywood than the boxing ring. It appealed, I suppose, to that working-class instinct that 'might is right', and echoed the cry of every young lad, picked on by another: "Well, anyway, my Dad could lick your Dad any day!" After all, didn't Rockfist Rogan, that comic-book hero whose exploits we read about every week on the front of "The Champion" comic, not only beat the wicked Hun in thrilling aerial combat, but also gave them split lips and cauliflower ears in the ring, into the bargain?

Actually, it was from comics that we gained most of our role models, and the outlet for our longing for some conspicuous success in the world was in sport. We lapped up stories of Alf Tupper, the working-class kid who beat all the nobs on the running track, of Limp-Along Leslie, who played football for England in spite of his handicap, and of Wilson, the mysterious ageless man, who excelled at every sport he turned his hand to. We, too, spent all our waking hours playing games. We lived in the street, and the early childhood games, the hopscotch, marbles, skipping and roller skating developed later on into a society that revolved about ball games. The little kids honed their throwing and catching skills playing "Queenie", which automatically led on to the fast chasing games such as "Hot Rice", "Cannon" or "Stick", which needed sophisticated throwing and catching skills. We always took a ball with us everywhere we went, even to the cinema, so that we could practise our ball skills during the walk there and back.

We soon graduated from throwing the ball long distances from end to end of the street to each other, to other variations of the throw and catch routine. My mother was driven absolutely frantic by the constant pounding of the ball against the wall of the house above the entry, or in the piece of wall between the kitchen window and the dining-room window at the back, while we practised throwing and catching, and a multitude of variations of throwing a ball against a surface and catching it as it came back. My brother and I perfected the skill of each standing in one of the gardens, front or back, and throwing the ball over the house to each other, counting points for how many times we actually caught it.

Next came team games: cricket on the pavement at the corner of the road, with the street lamp serving as one set of wickets and the pig-bin (that throwback to the war-time motto of "waste not, want not", which lingered well into the post-war years of austerity), as the other. In those early days I never mastered the subtleties of the game. I could never accept being the batsman left in when my last partner was out and yet being unable to continue batting, or the idea that my brother's aim, as bowler, was to hit the wickets and get me out, not to hit my bat and thus enable me to make a lot of runs. We played football in winter, out in the street, under the fitful gleam of the street lamp, until our mothers forced us indoors, and on Sunday mornings we sometimes wandered up to the park, where the morning football matches had left the pitches ankle-deep in the sort of mud that is supposed to do wonders for the complexion. There we played with real goalposts, real pitch markings and real mud. I, being a girl, always had the distinct disadvantage of wearing a skirt, usually some totally inappropriate garment, inconveniently tight and usually in some embarrassingly bright colour, which had to be tucked unceremoniously into my knickers, to enable me to make all the spectacular dives and leaps essential to any goalkeeper. I was forced to play in goal after I had once tackled Tony (who lived opposite me), sending him flying over the fence into Mrs Wilson's hedge. I was thus labelled 'dangerous' and obliged to play in goal, where I could do less damage. I didn't mind: I'd play anywhere, as long as I could play. After sessions in the park I would return home for Sunday dinner, dripping with mud, my school shoes caked in mud, which added an inch to my height and gave me the weighted boots of the deep-sea diver. These had to be hidden from Mom until the mud had dried and could be scraped off with one of Mom's best dinner knives, ready to do duty again as school shoes, come Monday morning.

As a matter of fact, my being accepted into the society of the street, into playing all the games the boys played, was remarkable, and by no means universal. Girls did skipping, hopscotch, Queenie, but not the more boisterous boys' games, and certainly not football. There was a local lad who used to pass our road on his way to the park for football practice, who was filled with shuddering horror at the thought of playing with a girl. His name was Sam, and he had one of those faces that looked old before its time. He wore cut-down adults' clothes, the heavy boots of the working man and the short back and sides haircut of his elders, with a little knot of would-be curls on top, tamed into mere undulations by the application of copious amounts of tap-water. He had the chiselled face of working-class resignation to his lot and the working-class man's scorn of females, and it was clear that he'd rather die than be seen playing with a girl.

And, really, Sam's attitude was the prevailing one of the time. Boys might well take a girl to the pictures or to the dance-hall when they were courting, but after marriage, the sexes followed their own pastimes, rigidly segregated. Men chose those pastimes that would get them away from women, who were looked upon as a necessary evil. Even their pubs had men-only 'Smoke Rooms' or bars, into which no woman of any reputation would go. Then there was fishing, which took them away for weekends, far from any female influence. My dad used to go away for weekends to Bewdley, fishing in the River Severn. Actually, what went on there we never found out, for he never brought home any fish for the pot, although he had a convincing fund of stories along the lines of 'the one that got away'. Once, in the season, we were overjoyed to be brought back a large basket of cherries, though I did wonder at the time what connection there was between them and the river. But these expeditions were a closely guarded male secret. While their menfolk were away, the women whiled away the time looking after the kids and going to the cinema, where they drooled over their celluloid heroes, whose glamorous and scandalous lives they read about every week in "Picturegoer" and "Pictureshow" magazines. Even football was an exclusively male pursuit. Men took their sons to the match, and even men in their thirties often went to the games with their own boys and their fathers, but girls were not welcome. Any man taking his wife or his daughter to a match would be looked upon as a dangerous radical, a traitor to his sex, allowing women into the exclusively male world of football.

After the Second World War, there was a great upsurge of interest in football, with all the men returned from the war and longing to get back to 'normal' life, which included football. Gates were enormous: even in the Second Division, West Bromwich had gates of 45,000 in 1947 to see Southampton, and 48,000 to see Newcastle, while Wolves, in the First Division, had 53,000 to see them play Derby and 53,000 for a game against Grimsby. But amongst these vast crowds there were hardly any females. A look at newsreel pictures of the time shows huge banks of men and boys, cloth-capped and mufflered, row upon row of drably dressed, neatly arranged men, standing on great tiers of terracing, open to the elements, silhouetted at the back of the vast sea of humanity against the sky, swaying in unison when the action got exciting, but orderly, restrained, as disciplined as they had been in their war years in the army, returned now to civvy life, to the ramshackle football stadia, boasting no facilities, that they regarded as their birthright.

Yet, to females, a sport that counted its devotees in millions, and which filled stadia all over the country every weekend, was virtually unknown. Indeed, when Johnny Nicholls, great stalwart of the West Bromwich team, tried to impress a girl at the local palais, the Adelphi in West Bromwich, by saying to her with affected nonchalance, "I'm Johnny Nicholls, you know," it was no real surprise when the young lady replied, with no spark of recognition, "Pleased to meet you. I'm Doris Jones"! Among the cognoscenti the legendary names of Matthews, Finney, Lawton, and Mannion had an aura of divinity, but to their wives, sisters and girl friends, they, for the most part, meant nothing. All they knew was that every Saturday their men went off to the match, which they discussed in the pub with their mates over the next week. There was no glory-chasing: men supported their

local team through thick and thin, and rivalry was very local indeed
– Liverpool/Everton, Birmingham/Villa, United/City – and all the
more passionate for that.

Football was much discussed in our house: my dad was a
Birmingham supporter. He'd been a fine footballer in his youth,
asked to turn professional when he was seventeen, but had chosen to
stick to his trade as a metal spinner because, he explained to me, " In
those days, the League was very rough and I had no guarantee that I
wouldn't end up in a couple of years with a broken leg and no trade
to fall back on." His best mate was Cyril Trigg, who played fullback
for the Blues, and they all met up at weekends at their local, The
Grange. (Its full title was "St Bernard's Grange", but 'the Grange' it
always was to those in the know). Cyril Trigg's daughter, Brenda, was
in my class at Junior School but I never actually met her Dad, he was
just my dad's mate, remote and unknowable. My dad didn't watch
his team play very often, using as his excuse when I asked him why
not, "Well, they never came to see me when I was bad!" but,
nevertheless, Blues were always his team.

Strangely enough, my brother was entirely atypical of working-
class boys in general in that he was totally uninterested in sport. He
played cricket with me in Gran's garden, felling Grandad's prized
gladioli with injudicious square cuts, but there were no male bonding
sessions between him and my dad on the terraces of St Andrews.
Actually, just after the war, when toys couldn't be got for love nor
money, Dad, determined that my brother should bring glory to the
name of Nash on the football field, managed, (how, I don't know), to
acquire for him a real leather football, full-sized and with the now
legendary knobbly leather lace, guaranteed to give you concussion
whenever you headed it, and to get as stodgy as a Christmas pudding
when played with on a muddy pitch. Instead of being overjoyed and
proud, as my father had fondly imagined he would be, my brother
showed no interest whatever in the wondrous gift, and it was I who
swooped on it with whoops of joy, and ultimately wore it out in
battles to the death in the street and over the park, leaving my father
bewildered and disappointed.

There was, you see, no leeway in the appropriateness of toys for
the different sexes. I was regularly, and infuriatingly, bought by

relatives, dolls, prams, girls' baking sets, toy tea-sets and the like, all the required appurtanences of the 'little homemaker', while my brother received toy cars, guns, lethal-looking bows and arrows, and a chemistry set, which presented unlimited potential for causing havoc. I was even made to give up a toy fire-engine, that I'd bought with some birthday money, to a male cousin, and to accept in exchange some more appropriate gift, more appropriate, that is, to the stereotypical girl. I was made to feel a second-class citizen: my role was fixed, boring, unfulfilling, set in the stone of tradition and I was to just get on with accepting it. But that was reckoning without the influence of football.

It wasn't just the putting down of girls into set roles that depressed me, though: life at home was stifling and depressing for more than just this. For six days of every week we teetered on the edge of financial disaster. Money came into the house on Friday, pay-day, and was gone by Saturday, leaving us to struggle through the rest of the week as best we could, with the help of the pawn shop and food on the slate from the local grocery store. Everybody on our estate seemed to accept this hand-to-mouth existence as inevitable. They saw nothing beyond the traditionally circumscribed life of the working classes. The boys saw nothing beyond leaving school at fifteen, working long hours in a factory, marrying young to a local girl, then spending the rest of their lives in the daily grind of providing for a wife and family, with only fishing, football and the pub at weekends to make life bearable. For the girls it would be a couple of years working in a factory, or, at best, a shop, before early marriage, children and the perennial problems of how to make ends meet, with only Hollywood make believe at the cinema as a bit of escape from the monotony of the daily round. This, I promised myself, wasn't going to be my lot. I was going to cross the divide, get out of the rut I seemed destined for: and my first way out, I decided, was to be through the forbidden world of football.

CHAPTER 2

Follow The Dream

My resolution made, the first question centred on just how I was going to go about breaking into this male stronghold. My dad wouldn't take me to matches: he'd be seen as a traitor to his sex if he turned up to matches with a girl in tow. Anyway, he didn't want me there, reporting back to Mom what went on and how he spent his money. I couldn't go by myself: although we children were left to our own devices for weeks and years while our parents were at work, and I was left to mind the children and run the house from an early age, for some reason my parents considered it unsuitable for me to go to a football match by myself until I was well into my teens. Housemaid, cook, cleaner, nanny and skivvy were entirely appropriate activities for a young girl to accomplish on her own, it appeared, but to go to a football match and stand on the terraces with crowds of men, was too risky a pastime, even for a girl raised in the rough-and-tumble of the streets of a Council estate. So, for a while, I was forced to bide my time. I played football in the street, I played football all the way to the bus-stop when I started at the Grammar School, I perfected my ball control skills in the garden, and I waited.

While I waited, I idolised the incomparable Stanley Matthews. He was my first football hero and my early scrapbooks have nothing but pictures of him in them. The passion was highlighted, if not kindled, by the so-called "Matthews Cup Final" of 1953. We didn't have a television ourselves, but our neighbour across the road rented one specially for the occasion, such was the fervour to see if Matthews could at last win the Cup Winners' medal that had eluded him thus far. Even our neighbour's imagination was fired by the sheer drama of this last tilt at the one honour that he had missed in a career filled with glittering triumph. Twice he'd been to Wembley, only for Blackpool to be beaten. In 1948 they'd lost to Johnny Carey's Manchester United and in 1951 it had been Jackie Milburn's Newcastle that had thwarted his ambition. Of course, sportsman that he was, he said they had nothing to be sorry about, for they'd reached

Wembley twice in four years, but we knew better. We felt that it was his due that the game should offer him every honour it had to bestow. After all, genius deserves it. It's all very well to have poetry written in your honour, to have poet Alan Ross describe you as "trim as a yacht, with similar lightness ...... improving like wine with age", but it didn't compare to a Cup Winners' medal, did it? And we were willing him to get it. Even my mother, hardly given to sentimental gestures, bought for me from the local newsagent's shop, when she called in to buy a paper, a copy of 'Football Monthly', which had an action picture of my hero on the back, in full colour, to grace my bedroom wall until it finally fell to pieces, colours faded and corners dog-eared.

Stanley Matthews

Come the afternoon of the game, we all crowded into Mrs Butler's front room, the football fans, the uninvited and the merely curious alike, all eyes fixed unerringly on the box in the corner, by the fireplace, with its small screen and hazy picture. Soon it would be repossessed by the TV company, for lack of payment of the rental, but it was safe for this day at least. United as we all were in the cause of Matthews' winner's medal, we were a seething mass of despair when Bolton went into a 3-1 lead, (however deserved this was), and we were already in our imaginations wringing our hands in the anguish of yet another defeat for Blackpool, the third in six years. Then came the transformation for which we'd all been praying, though with little hope of success, which just served to illustrate most graphically the callousness of blind partisanship. A Bolton player was injured, and, with no substitutes allowed, limped on, ineffective, on the wing. From that moment the tide turned. Pop-eyed and sweaty-palmed we watched as Blackpool hauled themselves back into the game and, when the scores were level, 3-3, with only a couple of minutes to go, we all resembled wrung-out dishcloths, writhing in our chairs, barely able to watch. The commentator was just saying, "I don't think the faint hearts can stand extra time," while Mrs Butler slumped weakly in her chair, fanned by her youngest with a folded copy of "The Daily Mirror", when Matthews raced down the right wing, crossed the ball to the waiting Bill Perry, who joyfully slammed it into the net. The room erupted with shouts of jubilation. What did we care that ten men had lost to eleven? What did we care that scoring the winning goal had been Bill Perry's only contribution of any note to the match? He was still a hero. What if Bolton had been the better side? Matthews had his

Bill Perry,
scorer of Blackpool's winner.

medal. It was his day. Stan Mortensen had scored a hat-trick, but he got scarcely a mention: there was only one man that had played that day. Mortensen scored three goals but it was still "The Matthews Cup Final". Years later, when Stan Mortensen died, a wag at his funeral described it with irony as "The Matthews Funeral", which just about sums up the total unfairness of blinkered partisanship, something I was going to know a lot about as I joined the ranks of long-suffering football supporters.

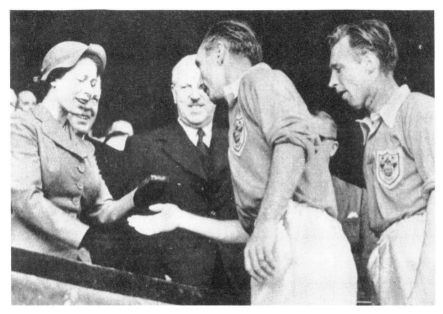

Matthews gets his winner's medal at last.

After the excitement of the Final, Mrs Butler's television went back to the rental company and I returned to keeping in touch with football via the radio and "Sports Report", which brought not only the results but interviews with players and comments by experts on the game. After the war there had at first been no sports programme on Saturday, merely the reading of the results after the news, but in the late forties came the early version of "Sports Report", which went out from 5.30 to 6.00pm on Saturday evening. By the time I became addicted to the silver voice of Eamonn Andrews, however, the programme had been extended to an hour, from 5.00 to 6.00pm. It was a national institution, reflecting the national obsession with football, allowing us to hear not just the plain results, but the stories behind the scores, the players' views and those of the managers.

Funnily enough, in those days, managers were not generally nationally known figures, and very few appeared regularly on the radio. Indeed, it was rare for club managers even to have their own page in the match programme, where they might exhort the supporters to stick by the team in a lean patch and explain why last week's match was lost. Leicester City had a page given over to their manager's thoughts, with a picture of Matt Gillies and his signature at the end of the piece, but it was rare. In these days of managers' changing almost weekly, in the ongoing game of musical chairs, it might be a practice worth adopting by clubs keen to prevent embarrassment or reprinting costs. Just putting the manager's name at the top of the page, with those of Directors, Secretary and other officials, might be a discreet way of distracting attention from the next scapegoat for the team's failings.

Matt Gillies says . . .

I DID not see Leicester City's match at Old Trafford on Saturday as I had other club business to attend to—running the rule over a player who has been recommended to us.

This player did not impress me very greatly, but no one can be judged on a single showing. And in any case it does not follow that a club will make a bid for a player because they are interested in him. There is much more to be done before the talk gets around to terms.

I was pleased to see we have got a home draw in the Third Round of the F.A. Cup—and against very good friends of ours—Lincoln City. Oddly enough they are having the same sort of League troubles as we are at present, but we can both cast those aside on January 10th and concentrate on the Cup.

Speaking of League troubles, let me remind you that last season Lincoln seemed to be certain to go down into Division Three, but they WON THEIR LAST SIX GAMES and escaped.

That not only shows what can be done: it illustrates a fact that so many people forget—you are never down until the last whistle blows.

The manager speaks!
Leicester City

The managers of the two best teams of the era, Matt Busby of Manchester United and Stan Cullis of Wolves, featured regularly on "Sports Report", but most managers were shadowy figures, known only to their local fans, certainly not the horned and cloven hooved monsters that they are so often portrayed as being these days, who must be sacrificed with monotonous regularity, to ensure the survival of their struggling teams. Human sacrifice, so soon after the war, was, in the 1950s, out of favour.

Actually, to the ordinary football fan, managers didn't seem to have any really important function to perform, apart from making sure that the team trained and were fit enough to play, picking the team for the week and pinning up the team sheet on Saturday morning. After all, there was no important wheeler-dealing to be done, no million pound transfer deals to arrange, since all the players were paid the same amount and to move from one team to another hardly made much sense. In the 1950s, indeed, the record transfer fee only rose from the £30,000 that "the Bank of England" team, Sunderland paid Villa for Trevor Ford, to the £45,000 that Manchester United paid for Albert Quixall in 1958. Neither were there any new and revolutionary new tactics for the manager to dream up in the fifties. We never needed, as supporters, to complain about the manager's changing the 4-4-2 system to a sweeper system, or a flat back four, or castigate him for putting his faith in man-to-man marking. As far as we were concerned, there was only one system – the W formation, which, with five forwards up against only two fullbacks and a centre half, was all about scoring goals. Nothing much else mattered.

Of course, you needed a good goalkeeper, a model of athleticism, who could fling himself cat-like across the goal, making spectacular saves from shots with 'goal' written all over them. But, as for full-backs, they were just the journeymen of the team, necessary, but not worth paying a lot of money for. Nobody went to a match to see the fullbacks. They were expected to loiter in the last quarter of the field and be the rocks upon which the darting runs of slippery wingers foundered. They took the ball from the opposing winger, then booted it upfield, (preferably to a colleague, though this was not obligatory). When the cry went up, "Get rid of it!", they did, then they hung about, waiting for the winger to try his luck again. They did not venture over the half-way line; that was foreign territory, and should a fullback actually score a goal, the attention of the press would be guaranteed! It wasn't until Alf Ramsey came along that people saw that a fullback didn't have to be just a stopper; he could be a constructive player who turned defence into attack. Ramsey's ability to pass accurately, to turn defence into attack in one sweeping movement, burst upon a startled world and paved the way, I suppose, for today's wing-backs, which combine attack and defence in the same player.

Alf Ramsey

By the 1950s the days of the attacking centre-half had gone, killed off by Stan Cullis, stopper par excellence. They became, with the fullbacks, the heart of the defence. The hub of the team, the creative dynamo, were the wing-halves, who took the ball from defence and turned it into attack, spraying sweeping, forty yard passes crossfield to the wingers, or feeding the other artists of the team, the inside forwards, whose job it was to service the centre-forward and the wingers, all of whom scored the bulk of the goals.

Wingers stayed on the wing, waiting for passes, whereupon they galloped down the touchline to the dead ball line, before unleashing inch-perfect crosses to the big, brave, strong centre-forward, whose job it was to lash it into the net. Wingers scored goals, too, but the supporters expected them to wait patiently on the wing for service. Starve them of service, of course, and they were effectively out of the game. Woe betide any winger, starved of the ball, who wandered inside to look for it, only for a colleague to pass to where he was confidently expected to be, only for the ball to run harmlessly into touch. "Stop on your wing!" would be the enraged cry from the terraces, and, experiment made, the winger would retreat sheepishly to the touchline.

With the roles within the team so rigidly defined, with players staying with their local club often for their whole playing career, with no great negotiations about contracts or transfers to carry on, it's no wonder managers were hardly known to spectators. It was hard for us to imagine exactly what they did. They didn't, on the face of it, seem to have a great influence on the team; they were just back-room figures, like coaches or trainers. I was at a boxing promotion once, at the Albert Hall, when Manager, Terry Lawless, between rounds, climbed into the ring, bent over his fighter, his face a few inches from the perspiring face of his protege, exhorting and advising. Seeing this spectacle, the old man next to me opined, to no-one in particular, "That Terry Lawless, 'e 'ypnotises 'em, 'e does. They're like zombies wiv 'im." We didn't see that kind of effect produced by football managers. All their work went on behind closed doors, and as far as we were concerned, they didn't do anything much.

Nowadays, of course, their faces constantly adorn our television screens, making fatuous remarks about taking every game as it comes, admitting that the opposition had made it difficult for them, and opining sagely that there's a long way to go before the end of the season, but the lads won't let him down. Now, we see them ad nauseam during matches, sitting on the bench watching the action, while we watch them looking worried or anguished, scratching their noses, yawning or making learned notes, while, on the pitch, the action continues, unseen by the viewing public.

But in the fifties there was nothing of this, only the radio. A few minutes before 5 on Saturday evening I'd position myself in the crowded, cluttered kitchen, as near to the radio as possible, between the dresser and the fireplace, where hissed a steaming, spluttering mass of cabbage stalks and potato peelings, heaved onto the back of the fire to make the coal go further and which filled the kitchen with a smoky smell and a haze that lasted for days. Then came the reading of the results, with the elation or despair that inevitably accompanied them, before it was time to get off to the local shop for the pink "Sports Argus", which not only gave the results but reports of the matches and pictures of the action.

Meanwhile, I had to make some decisions. After all, I couldn't go on like this, living vicariously through reading the paper or listening to the radio. I actually had to go to matches. So, I turned my attention to persuading my father that I really was old enough to go by myself. Dripping water finally wears away stone, so they say, and

in the end he agreed to my going to watch Birmingham City play.
Finally, in the 1954-5 season, I was to become a real football fan, at
last. What had caused my father to be so squeamish about allowing
me to go to a football ground, I don't know, for he'd never to my
knowledge, either before or since, shown the least interest in my
activities, but it was my tough luck that he'd chosen just this moment
to play at being the concerned parent. Still, it was churlish to
complain, now that he'd relented, and on February 5, 1955, I went to
my first Football League match. Of course, there were no drums, no
trumpets, no fanfares, just a typically scrambling affair between two
Second Division teams, Birmingham and Lincoln, a game that
finished 3-3. What the game did do was cement the time-honoured
football fan's belief that their side, even in a draw, were morally the
victors, for Birmingham had the ball in the net twice more, only for
both efforts to be ruled offside, which sent me home with the firm
belief that, morally, we had won.

Standing on the draughty terraces, with ugly concrete walls and
metal barriers, on a chill February afternoon, merely whetted my
appetite for more Titanic struggles to come, and such was my
excitement at having reached a personal milestone in my life – access
to the forbidden territory – that my programme, clutched
convulsively in my frozen little hand at moments of high tension, had
been reduced to a state of ugly corrugation, creased and slightly
grubby. When I got home, I toyed with the idea of ironing it, to
restore it to its former pristine state, but as we still used in our house
the old-fashioned flat irons, heated on a gas jet, then picked up with
a pad of folded cloth and applied to the garment, I was much afraid
it might be too hot and would set fire to my precious programme. So
it is that it survives, corrugations and all.

My first experience of professional football had enthused me for
more, and later in February I paid 2/- to see Birmingham play
Doncaster in the Third round of the Cup. I had hoped to see the new
wonder-kid, eighteen year old Allick Jeffrey play for Doncaster, but
he was injured, but I did see Charlie Williams, later to make a living
on the Halls as a comedian. Judging by the cries of "You great
clown!' that come up from the terraces on a Saturday afternoon, it's
perhaps, a profession that many footballers might excel in! Anyway,

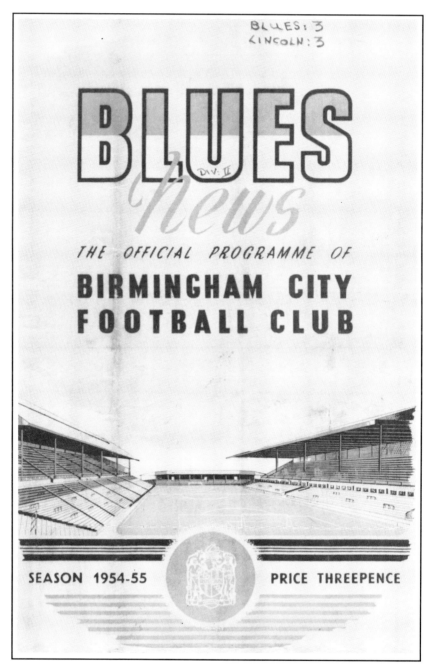

My first match!

Birmingham won the match and I came away pleased that my team hadn't lost either of the matches I'd seen them play. I looked forward to the future with optimism: all I needed now was a football scarf. Now, unfortunately for me, money and I were complete strangers to one another, and I couldn't for the life of me see how I was going to raise enough money to buy a scarf. The only way, as I saw it, was to make such a nuisance of myself to my mother, wheedling and cajoling, particularly on pay-day, when her money would be burning a hole in her purse, that she'd fork out for a scarf, just to get rid of me. For a couple of weekends this cunning plan was a dismal failure: she merely whacked me with the broom she was using to sweep the yard and told me to clear off.

Blues 2   Doncaster 0

On the third week, however, the ploy worked; not until late afternoon, but she finally cracked. Trouble was, I hadn't got time to go into town in search of a scarf, and I couldn't think of any local shop that was likely to have one. In desperation, I took a bus to a local area which boasted a row of rather dispiriting-looking shops, where I came upon a somewhat dismal, old-fashioned shop that sold school uniforms, grey short trousers, blazers in drab colours and school caps. It was one of those boring, respectable shops, with goods in wooden trays under the counter and in little cupboards at the back, behind the counter, nicely folded and graded according to size and colour. It didn't seem at all the sort of shop that would have anything as vulgar as a football scarf, but I hadn't gone all that way for nothing, so I went inside. A bell ting'd and a lady came out from the back room, a quiet middle-aged lady in a dark two-piece. She looked disapprovingly at me and asked frostily what I wanted. Five minutes later I emerged, clutching a blue and white woolly scarf. It was the wrong blue: I knew that. It was navy blue, more the colour of West Brom than the royal blue of Birmingham City, but I'd bought it because it was all they had, and if I'd taken the money back to Mom it would have just disappeared, along with my chance of ever owning a scarf. I wore it, of course, but I knew it wasn't right, and from that moment my relationship with the Blues went downhill.

CHAPTER 3

The Fifties

The 1955-56 season.

What came between me and the Blues was another team. The Wolves had won the First Division Championship in the 1953-4 season, which had given them a high profile, and the newspapers and radio were full of the great exploits of this wonder team. What confirmed them, however, as the glamour team of the age was the fact that they had had the foresight to install floodlights long before everyone else, which enabled them to stage glamorous night matches against foreign opposition. Innovation in football is generally slow to come, but Wolves had installed their floodlights as early as 1953, while Birmingham didn't follow suit until 1956, West Brom in 1957 and the Villa not until 1958. What ultimately decided teams that floodlights were a good idea was the experience of Birmingham and West Brom at the beginning of January 1957. West Brom, who didn't have floodlights, were forced to play a Cup replay against Doncaster during the afternoon, which restricted the gate to 18,000. On the same day, however, Birmingham, who had floodlights, met Carlisle in a Cup replay of their own, in the evening under lights, which attracted a gate of over 60,000. I was there that evening, at a packed St Andrews, hanging from the girders at the back of the terraces, looking down on a huge blue sea of spectators, swaying to the rhythm of the emotion, all eyes focused on the pitch, dotted with tiny figures who wove intricate patterns on the green carpet. After the exhilaration of the noise, the excitement and the victory, I slipped out and went home. My dad, who had been in the thick of the seething mass of fans, didn't get home until midnight, such was the crush! It was the Wolves, though, who were the floodlight kings, attracting to Molineux glamorous foreign sides that were virtually unknown to English fans. Best of all came Honved, from Hungary, fielding many of the players that had recently humiliated England 7-1 and 6-3. Such was the interest in seeing them and Moscow

Spartak, that the matches were televised live and still attracted gates of 55,000. Thus, during the fifties, Wolves were hot news, and this proved to be my undoing, for all the publicity brought to my attention the Wolves captain, Billy Wright, with whom I immediately fell in love, which changed my football life for ever. Of course, my dad expected me to stick to the Blues through thick and thin and yet I defied him and defected to the Wolves.

Billy Wright

My own first reaction to this act of treason was one of dismay, but it was a passion, both for the man and the team, that endures to this day, for, as every football fan knows, fantasy can always outstrip boring, inconvenient, prosaic reality. I was, nonetheless, deeply ashamed. It looked so much like glory-chasing, supporting Wolves, who won things, and rejecting Birmingham, who never won anything. Worse, it looked so mortifyingly 'girlie', supporting a team just because you fancied one of the players. There seemed to be something shamefully female about it, somehow, letting a man interfere with the serious business of football. I couldn't believe my own stupidity, risking my credibility as a serious football supporter by letting my emotion rule. But, then, football is wholly to do with emotion, isn't it, and I could hardly ignore mine. It wasn't as if foot-ballers in general could muster enough glamour to turn a girl's head. These days, with young footballers earning small (and sometimes large) fortunes, strutting about on the catwalk, modelling fashions and tempting every half good-looking girl to try her luck with this new breed of eligible bachelor, such nonsense might be understandable, but then, even Billy Wright, Captain of England, was paid a mere pittance and lived, like all the unmarried players, in approved lodgings, cossetted by a motherly landlady, who would see that they got good, wholesome food and plenty of early nights.

No, it was no good, I had to support Wolves, and although my father wouldn't let me go to matches in Wolverhampton, I worshipped them from afar. I actually had the chance of a ticket to the Honved match, but this time it was my mother who ruined my life, for my younger sister had whooping cough, which I hadn't had, so the strict rules of quarantine decreed that I had to stay indoors for a month. In vain did I wheedle and threaten: I could not go out, and certainly not to a football ground, so I sat with very bad grace, crouched by the radio, cursing my luck and my little sister, and trying not to cry tears of sheer disappointment, while I listened to the commentary on the thrilling match on the radio and drank in the excitement second-hand. I couldn't even see it on television, for we didn't have a set.

A broken heart doesn't last for ever, though, and by the beginning of the 1955-6 season I was finally allowed to go to Wolverhampton and watch the Wolves. All through the summer I'd cut out from the newspapers everything about the club – pictures of them in Russia, playing Moscow Dynamo and Spartak, to packed houses of 70,000 people. Such was the interest created by this trip abroad that I was moved to spend a whole 6d on a book about Soviet football, which must be something of a collectors' item now. Then they returned, to begin the season in which, at last, I was to be a real Wolves supporter.

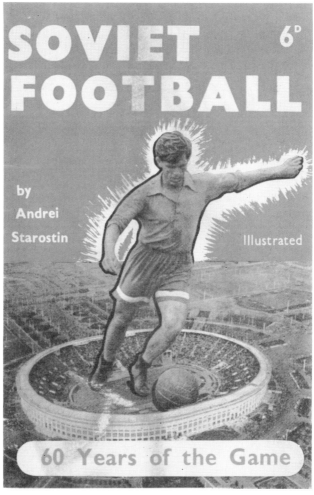

Secrets of Russian football!

Wolves v Moscow Dymano in Moscow 1955

Supporting a team miles from home brought me several headaches, the first being how on earth I was going to raise enough money to get to Wolverhampton to see the matches. The spectre of destitution stared me in the face throughout my childhood. I walked miles before I caught the bus to school, to save the extra penny fare. I couldn't go out much in the evening because I couldn't raise the bus fare to go into town and, anyway, I'd have to borrow a pair of shoes from my mother, as I only had my school shoes. But, where there's a will there's a way, so they tell us, and for me it was Wolverhampton or bust! If he remembered and it had been a good week, my dad gave me 7/6d pocket money a week, and the whole of this was inevitably squandered on a trip to Wolverhampton on a Saturday, and total immersion in being a Wolves supporter, which, in my mind, I equated with being one of the angels who sat on the right hand of the Almighty, but which also meant that I'd be totally penniless for the rest of the week.

Getting companions to worship at the shrine with me, however, was entirely another matter. I sometimes coerced a schoolfriend into accompanying me. She was an easygoing girl, absolutely uninterested in football in general and the Wolves in particular, but she tagged along, as uncomplaining as a pet dog, and spent the afternoon standing on the terraces, placidly knitting, completely oblivious to the life and death dramas that were working themselves out like Greek tragedies on the pitch before her. Today she'd never be allowed in with lethal weapons such as knitting needles, but then she was a common sight, turning out intricate woolly garments by the minute as the time ticked by to full-time, totally unaware of her surroundings. When she couldn't be persuaded to come with me, I sometimes, on the promise of a day out and a ride on a train, got my younger sister to oblige. She was no more interested in football than my schoolfriend, but she was willing to suffer anything for a day out, away from the warring factions at home. She never took her knitting, (her knitting, like mine, always had a tendency to gain length without breadth and generally ended up as a scarf, stuffed in a junk-filled draw at home and left to moulder unseen), but she did have a novel way of combatting the elements on the Molineux terraces, for she once took off her gloves and put them on her feet, to keep out the cold from the lying snow, whilst waiting for the end of the match and a trip on a warm train.

My first match of the 1955-6 season, however, didn't involve the Wolves at all. On September 10th I made the long journey to Villa Park, to see my hero, Stanley Matthews, play. I went into town by bus, then waited in an enormous queue to catch one of the fleet of Football Special buses that ferried the supporters out to Villa Park, on the other side of town. These fleets of special buses were a common sight in those days, for, with so few people owning cars, everybody travelled by bus. For a while the whole town centre would be taken over by vast armies of football fans, patiently queuing in huge lines that stretched all along Colmore Row, waiting their turn to board one of the long line of buses, bearing the exciting legend "Villa Park" on their destination blinds.

Once I had found my inexpert way onto the terraces of this unfamiliar ground I settled in amongst the Villa supporters and prepared to shout for Blackpool, thus attracting the enmity of the Villa faithful. I survived the experience, in spite of getting into something of a noisy confrontation with a strident Irishman, claret and blue eyed, and crazy as far as I could see, who really seemed to believe that McParland and Hickson were the equals of Matthews and Mortensen, but at the end I got out unscathed, with honours even. And the teams also drew, 1-1.

Then the season began in full earnest and I set out to support my own team, bubbling over with excitement at the thought of setting foot at last within the holy shrine of Molineux. I'd never been to Wolverhampton, hadn't a clue where the ground was or what it would be like when I found it, but a friend from school and I approached the new experience with an excitement bordering on frenzy. We fashioned rosettes for the occasion out of bits of scrounged material, and if the yellow of the rosettes was a pale, anaemic primrose yellow instead of the required strong, vibrant gold of the Wolves, and if they were so shoddily constructed as to unravel at the first signs of agitation, then at least we had made the effort. In fact, when we got off the train in Wolverhampton one surprised native commented that you'd think it was a cup-tie, so festooned with the club colours were we. As a matter of fact, getting the club colours wrong haunted me all the way through. Not only had I got a Blues scarf that was the wrong blue, but also I never managed to capture the richness of the gold that was required for the Wolves. We bought a rattle and acquired from the Rag Market a bell, which we intended to paint in Wolves colours and take to matches, but when our milkman offered us some yellow paint to transform our purchases into Wolves fans, we found to our disappointment that it was the same watery primrose yellow that had characterised our ill-fated rosettes. Harbouring uncharitable thoughts about people who decorated their houses with such wishy-washy colours, I glumly set to to paint both bell and rattle with this eminently unsuitable colour, for I knew that anything remotely like the real thing was never likely to fall into my eager hands.

I had no more luck when I came to buy a suitable woolly scarf, for all I got was the now familiar pale yellow, with no hint of rich gold. Undeterred, I used yellow wool to embroider boldly on the scarf the names of my favourite players, and attached to it little plastic badges bearing the likenesses of the players, which could be bought from street vendors outside the ground on match days. Much later I was to discover that scarves of exactly the right colour could be bought from Jimmy Mullen's sports shop in Stafford Street, but I couldn't have both a new scarf and go to matches, so my inferior pale yellow and black specimen had to do. A few years later, one of my friends, whom I had persuaded to become a Wolves fan, bought one of Jim Mullen's scarves (she was at work and could easily afford it), then embroidered upon it the names of the players in finest gold embroidery silk, thus producing a wholly superior product to my own. It was soft, woolly, glowing with colour and class, embroidered neatly with tiny stitches, while mine was hard, cheap, crudely embroidered with wool and the wrong colour. Of course, it wouldn't have been the subject of real envy had we not once, while waiting for the players to emerge after the match, come across the motherly Mrs Colley, for many years Billy Wright's landlady, and had Mrs Colley not made a special point of going across to admire the workmanship of my friend's scarf, so neat and attractive. Now, for obvious reasons, Mrs Colley had to be cultivated and impressed, and at that moment, standing ignored in the background, I could cheerfully have pulled the admired scarf tight about my friend's neck and rendered her lifeless.

But, scarf or no scarf, my first visit to Molineux, in September 1955 was a patch of heaven in a life of infernal misery. I stood on the vast expanses of the South Bank, looked at the distinctive wooden gables of the right-hand stand, with the clock set in the middle, faced the fans on the smaller North Bank, and knew I was home. We were playing Chelsea and we won 2-1. The only fly in the ointment that day was that the man I'd particularly come to see, Billy Wright, wasn't playing, but I soon forgot my disappointment in the pleasure known to all football fans of finding fault with the opposition. At that time, Chelsea had two of the roughest and toughest fullbacks in Sillett and Willemse you could ever wish not to meet professionally and the treatment they meted out to our forwards ensured that I fermented in my heart a great hatred of Chelsea which has lasted forever. My dad's theory of defending was simple: if he gets past you, hack him down; but this philosophy offended my juvenile and undeveloped sense of fair play and I marked out Chelsea as candidates for consignment to the pains of hell. Even the chance to watch Frank Blunstone on the wing and Roy Bentley at centre forward couldn't render them palatable. My hatred became long-lasting and determined. I was almost tempted to remove the coloured picture of

Roy Bentley

Roy Bentley from my bedroom wall, where it took its place with the other heroes, culled from the pages of "Football Monthly", but I charitably reasoned that it wasn't his fault he played for Chelsea and generously left him where he was, between David Pegg of Manchester United and Len Shackleton of Sunderland. When, forty years later, Ruud Gullit brought his team of foreign artists to Stamford Bridge, to take the breath away with their wizardry, I almost forgave Chelsea for Willemse and Sillett – almost. But my first match with my new team had taught me one football lesson – that hatreds born of often unreasonable prejudice last for ever.

I couldn't go away with Wolves, of course – I couldn't raise the money – so I didn't entirely desert the Blues. I had a soft spot for them as they'd been the first professional side I'd seen, and anyway, they'd just been promoted to the First Division and I was curious to see how they'd cope in a higher grade of football, so on the weeks I didn't see Wolves, I went to St Andrews to see the Blues and renew acquaintance with the players I saw sometimes on my way home from school. Football players, paid very low wages, didn't often have cars and so generally used public transport, and as Blues owned some club houses that they let out to players and their families, in a road off the Coventry Road, along which I travelled to school, then many days we would find ourselves on the same bus as the players, returning home from training. It didn't seem very odd to us to find real-live heroes travelling on the same bus as the lowly fans – footballers were just ordinary, working-class men, with not much money, who drank in the same pubs as our dads and went to the same dance-halls as our big brothers and sisters. We regularly talked football with winger Gordon Astall and once I was rendered almost speechless to find myself sitting next to Noel Kinsey, Welsh international! I knew the Blues forward line of Astall, Kinsey, Brown, Murphy and Govan as well as I knew the Wolves': Hancocks, Broadbent, Swinbourne, Wilshaw and Mullen.

The first Blues match I saw that season was against Luton, who had been promoted with them. They'd had a bad start, with only two wins in seven matches, so a point against Luton in a dull 0 - 0 draw wasn't what they'd hoped for. Things went from bad to worse after this and it wasn't until the beginning of October that they got another win, this time against the stars of Spurs: 3-0, Blanchflower, Marchi, Ditchburn and Robb notwithstanding. It is one of the unwritten laws of football that London clubs are to be beaten at all costs, humiliated if at all possible, so the 3-0 scoreline was very satisfying even to me, who didn't really support Birmingham. It didn't last, though, for the next home game brought Sunderland and Len Shackleton. Shackleton was one of the enigmas of football, a players of mercurial temperament, quite capable of winning a match single-handed if he felt like it; equally capable of skulking on the wing for a whole match, making no effort to get the ball, even letting it run out of play when it was passed to him, if he didn't feel like running at that particular moment. He must have been a manager's nightmare, but he was a genius. At Birmingham that day, he was obviously feeling a little feeble, for he bestirred himself but twice, whereupon Sunderland scored two goals and won the match 2-1, after which the gaunt-faced, rather gormless-looking genius, bathed, dressed and went home.

Len Shackleton

After this defeat, my dad began to get a bit apprehensive, fearing that his team was going to tumble straight back down to the Second Division. He didn't actually go to the matches, you understand; the encouragement of his team was firmly placed in my hands, but he showed definite signs of alarm, which were soothed to some extent by a 5-0 defeat of Portsmouth away in their next match, in which Eddie Brown scored a hat-trick, which prompted my father to remark grudgingly, "Well, that's what he's there for, isn't it?" on the principle that it's better not to offer too much praise and encouragement, in case they let you down next week, as the inborn pessimism of the seasoned football fan naturally leads you to expect. Actually, in this case they didn't, for they beat Manchester City 4-3 at the end of October, which, unfortunately, wasn't an omen for the Cup Final to come the following May: but, then, the architect of Blues' downfall at Wembley, Don Revie, wasn't playing that day in October.

For the rest of the season I stood on the terraces at Birmingham, watching the Blues, in the first season after promotion, haul themselves to sixth place in the table, beating higher placed Arsenal and Manchester City on the way. But this season wasn't really to do with the league: for this season they got to Wembley for the Cup Final. They hadn't been in a final since they were beaten by West Brom in 1931, and my dad was caught up in the excitement of it all, since many of the old 1931 team had been friends of his. It started with a bang, trouncing Torquay 7-1 away, which so encouraged my dad that he went to Leyton Orient for the next round. He'd got the feeling, I suppose, that Blues were at last going to win something and eclipse the hated Villa, in whose shadow they had been for too long. On a foggy afternoon, when my dad saw the ball only twice, when it went out of play right near where he was standing, Blues won 4-0, although he had to ask someone who'd been standing at the other end what the score was at the end. That was it: he was hooked on following their progress. I wasn't allowed to go with him, of course. My job was to stand on the terraces and collect the tokens that were printed in the programmes, which, should the team finally make it to Wembley, could be exchanged for the right to buy a Cup Final ticket. The omens looked good when in the Fifth Round they beat West Brom, their conquerors in the 1931 final, and when they beat the mighty Arsenal 3-1 in the Sixth Round, the whole of blue Birmingham began to believe that this was, indeed, going to be their year. It was a feeling of hope and expectancy we hadn't had in Blues' fans for years. Blues, who'd never done anything, were going to get to Wembley and the effect on the city was remarkable. On the way to the tie at Arsenal, winger Alex Govan, had introduced into the sing-song on the team coach, the old Harry Lauder song, "Keep right on to the end of the road". Somehow, some passing supporters had heard it and when Blues were winning had burst into song. Thus, it became Blues' song, every bit as indisputably theirs as "You'll never

LEYTON: O
BLUES 4

OFFICIAL
PROGRAMME

LEYTON ORIENT
FOOTBALL CLUB LIMITED
LEYTON STADIUM, BRISBANE ROAD, LEYTON, E.10

PRICE
3D.

President : F. JOHN YOUNG, Esq.   Vice-President : H. F. ROBERTSON, Esq.
Chairman : H. S. ZUSSMAN, Esq.
Directors : F. F. Harris, Esq. (Vice-Chairman), C. Bent-Marshall, Esq., H. E. Lee, Esq.
Manager : ALEC W. A. STOCK   Secretary : A. H. R. HUGGETT
Medical Officer : Dr I. M. BELL   Telephone : LEY 1368

No. 33   **SATURDAY, 28th JANUARY, 1956**

Oriental Chatter
By " FORESTER "

GREETINGS one and all to Leyton Stadium.

* * * * *

A special welcome is extended to Birmingham F.C.—officials, players and supporters—for this afternoon's F.A. Challenge Cup fourth round tie.

It was in the corresponding round in January, 1952 that Orient scored a sensational 1—0 victory over Birmingham, at St. Andrew's, and thereby earned the right to a fifth round meeting with Arsenal, at Leyton Stadium. Orient lost that game by 3—0, but like today's clash with First Division Birmingham, the O's had everything to win and really nothing to lose in soccer prestige. They had already earned the label of " Giant Killers " for that season, and in their triumphant progress showed the utmost disregard for soccer reputations and fame. Such then is the F.A. Cup.

Our friends from Birmingham, perhaps, will hardly need reminding of that magnificent conquest of four years ago, but for Orient it is a cherished record. The winning goal was scored by little Tommy Harris, playing at centre-forward, but the man of the match

AN EPIC was the other Tommy in the Orient's side—Tommy Brown, who skippered and inspired the team at inside-left.

CUP-TIE

MEMORY On his day, Tommy Brown was the ideal soccer artist, and this was his day at St. Andrew's. Of the occasion I wrote in " Oriental Chatter " . . . . " Brown gave a showing that was talked of long afterwards. He was the perfect artist and architect, and when he is playing well there is none to better him. As a captain, too, he was " an inspiration."

Three members of that successful Orient team are playing today, Pat Welton, Les Blizzard and Stan Aldous. The side was : Welton ; Evans, Banner ; Blizzard, Aldous, Deverall ; Woan, Pacey, Harris, Brown, Blatchford. The same eleven played against the Arsenal afterwards.

Birmingham have, no doubt, planned to try to avenge that beating, and, believe me, Orient do not under-estimate the magnitude of their own task this afternoon. As champions of the Second Division last season, Birmingham have more than demonstrated their power and talents, and, indeed, have they not been tipped in many quarters as likely winners of the coveted F.A. trophy this season ?

If beaten fairly and squarely, Orient will not squeal. They will be the first to congratulate their conquerors, and wish them well in future battles to reach Wembley. However, Orient are determined fighters and on their own ground can usually produce their best against their best. Under the guidance of Manager Alec Stock, Orient players give their " all " all the time, and Mr. Stock has a fine cup record—Yeovil Town (5th round), then, Orient (fifth and sixth rounds). It is said he has " a knack of manœuvring " little ships " into ,harbours " safe from violent storms and raging seas." But, Mr. Stock says, the Orient cannot win matches alone, they must have the help of their supporters. And on that note I want to make an appeal to all loyal O's fans this afternoon. For goodness sake let your " hair down " and give the players encouragement. Let's have a Leyton roar. Please help the boys to achieve, and if things are going badly for them don't just give up the ghost, but exercise your vocal chords and shout ! The players will just love it.

* * * * *

Concensus of opinion is that Orient's 2—1 win over Brentford in last Saturday's league game here was just about one of their best successes. There were eleven heroes on the field from Pat Welton to unlucky Jack

STINGING Gregory, whose dislocated knee cap, forced him to switch from right-back to outside-left. It was truly a won-

" THE BEES " derful team effort, the sort of stuff which surely must make Orient fol-

AGAIN lowers very proud of the team and club they support. Gregory was an inspiration to his colleagues. His injury received in most unfortunate circumstances when the game was only four minutes old was enough to knock the life out of most sides, but not Orient. That old fighting spirit just had to come out. Trainer Les Gore told me that Gregory was in great pain, and after tending to the injury and

TODAY'S MATCH — K.O. 2.45 p.m.
BIRMINGHAM
(Fourth Round—F.A. Cup)

Leyton Orient programme
Orient 0 - Blues 4

walk alone" is the anthem of the Kop at Liverpool. So unusual was it for a song to be associated with a team then that in the programme for the match against Blackpool, after their semi-final win over Sunderland had made Wembley a certainty, there was inserted a personal message from the manager, Arthur Turner, in which he paid tribute to the effect the song had had on the players. He said hearing the song at the match "filled us all with emotion ... it was like a charm, and how much the players responded to it".

When the final whistle sounded at 4.40 p.m. last week I had tears of joy in my eyes, because of the success of our team, but also for the leading part that you, ' Our Supporters ' have played in any success we have gained. It has been beyond our wildest hopes, we thank you very sincerely and we owe you a debt. To repay you all, we will pick up where we left off last week, to bring the Cup back for you. This has been your fight as well as ours, and how you have fought for us, words fail me.

Last week at Sheffield, in the words of Sir Winston Churchill, " this was your finest hour."

' Our Song ' born in the coach on the way to play Arsenal in the Sixth Round, and sung by you all on Saturday last, filled us all with emotion. We thank you all, it was like a charm, and how much the players responded to it.

Having played in the Semi-Final and lost, I would pay tribute to our opponents from Sunderland, for the sporting and clean manner in which they played; the blow is more heavy when you are so near to Wembley. They all wished us well in the Final, and I am certain I voice the wishes of all our supporters for their future progress.

For the huge number of letters and telegrams I have received and the good wishes of all, I thank you most sincerely. I could not attempt to answer them all so please accept this as my reply to you.

With team spirit and co-operation by all, I am confident we can win the Cup.

ARTHUR TURNER, Manager.

Keep right on to the end of the road.

Dour, unfashionable Blues, so long the poor relations in football terms in Birmingham, were off to Wembley and cup fever scorched every corner of the town. Fortunately, Blues weren't my team, so when the time came for me to hand over my tokens to my dad, so he could get his ticket for the final, I didn't really mind, at least not until he came back after the match. Then I discovered that, by swapping

his cheap standing ticket in a pub for an expensive ticket for the stand, with a man who wanted to join his mates on the terraces, he'd managed to find himself sitting next to Stan Cullis, the manager of the Wolves. I was spitting mad. He'd talked to the great man! I'd got him a ticket and he'd met Stan Cullis! Proof, indeed, if proof were needed, of the innate unfairness of life.

That the Blues lost again is a fact of history. We watched them on the television, resplendent in their new strip, created specially for the occasion and willed them to win, but they were destroyed by a man using a wholly new tactical formation, Don Revie and his "deep lying centre-forward" ploy, a tactic that entirely foxed Birmingham and with which they never managed to come to terms. They never picked up Revie all afternoon and he destroyed them. My father reported that Stan Cullis had been disgusted by Birmingham's inability to adapt to new tactics, but they were new enough to

Wembley at last!

have undone better teams than Birmingham and though people turned out to see them come home without the cup, and although their song, "Keep right on ..." lingered for some years, they never reached such heights again, and my dad's interest in watching them waned.

In any case, in spite of the unprecedented excitement round our way for the Blues' exploits, this season belonged to the Wolves, as far as I was concerned. In the summer of 1955 I'd taken my 'O' levels and returned to school in the September to do my 'A' levels, with the intention of going to university after that. No-one before in our family had even been to a Grammar School, let alone to a university, so I would certainly be breaking new ground. My dad paid lip service to the idea of us all getting a good education, for he'd passed for the Grammar School himself, but had been unable to take up his place because his parents couldn't afford to buy the books he'd need, so he was quite willing for me to stay on at school as long as I liked. So was Mom, but for a different reason. She wanted me at home during the school holidays, to mind the younger children and run the home while she was out at work.

I hated school: I always had, ever since I'd started a couple of years late because I'd spent all my early childhood in hospital. I'd never settled into school and secondary school had proved to be no better. But I was smart enough to realise that if I was to escape the narrowness and poverty of my working-class background I needed an education, so I just soldiered on at school, wearing clipped to my school tie, under my regulation navy blue cardigan, badges of my football heroes, which could be looked at when lessons became too tedious. I even wrote to the Wolves' Secretary, the venerable J.T. Howley, asking if their club blazer badges could be bought by the general public. Even though I suffered all my schooldays from not wearing the correct uniform, standing out something alarming from the rest of my fellow pupils, I was quite willing to risk (yet again!), the wrath of our dreaded Senior Mistress, by replacing my boring school badge, a green interlaced WGS on a plain navy background, with the exciting Wolverhampton crest, bearing the legend, "Out of darkness cometh light". As it turned out, I was not called upon to make this great gesture of defiance and rebellion, for I received a polite little note from Mr Howley, informing me that the blazer badges were only issued to players and club officials, which patently didn't include me, so I just had to make do with my plastic badges of the players and wait for the weekend.

On match days I rose at crack of dawn, for there was the house to clean from top to bottom, all the grime of the week to be coaxed out of every room, shopping to be done, and the dinner prepared and put on to cook before I left home. I'd go to the station, tell the man I wanted a return to Wolverhampton. He always asked the same question, "Are you coming back today, love?" and on my answering in the affirmative, he'd hand over my ticket to freedom. As soon as I got to Wolverhampton I made for Jim Mullen's sports shop, where I'd try to get a few words with my hero before the match and could impress upon him the necessity of winning, otherwise I'd never hear the last of it from my dad. My mom had brought back from her job in a cafe a little ginger kitten, which I'd called Jim, in honour of Jim Mullen, but I never dared tell him of this singular honour, since the feline Jim turned out to be uncompromisingly thick, if strikingly handsome!

As a matter of fact, Jim Mullen was to prove something of a saviour to me, because he solved for me the virtually intractable problem of how to get hold of tickets for cup-ties. In order to get tickets you had to go personally to the ground and queue for them: postal applications weren't allowed. This, to me, meant disaster, for I couldn't raise the money to go twice to Wolverhampton, once to queue for tickets and once to go to the match. At first I experimented with going over to Wolverhampton on my brother's bike. My geography was not good, (I'd failed the subject at 'O' level), so I wasn't really at all sure of being able to find my way to Wolverhampton by road, but I solved the problem by asking a school friend (she of the knitting needles), who was doing Geography at 'A' level, to accompany me. She and her parents were cycling

Jimmy Mullen

fiends, belonging to the Cyclists' Touring Club and completing exhausting time trials and covering vast distances touring, her parents riding a quaint tandem and my friend astride her sturdy black bicycle, whose handlebars failed to face the front, thanks to her having once carelessly propped it up against the kerb in the street, whereupon it had fallen over into the road and been run over by a passing car.

We made it to the ground and I got my cup tickets, but this one single experience was enough to persuade me that all this bike-riding was too much like hard work and there must be an easier way to get hold of tickets. Before long, and to my relief, a solution to the problem presented itself, and from a most unexpected source. Jim Mullen, much impressed by my devotion to the Wolves when I lived such a long way away, offered to send me tickets by post for cup matches, and so it was arranged that he would send me the tickets and I would go to his shop on matchdays and pay him for them. Thus was my life, or at least my aching limbs, saved.

Sometimes, on the train to Wolverhampton I would meet up with a crowd of men, who got on the train at Tipton. They, really tickled by the novelty of a girl supporter, adopted me, taking me under their wing, buying me food and even paying my entrance fee for the match, which was tantamount to me to manna from heaven, for generally speaking I didn't eat at all on Saturdays, for I didn't have time to eat before I left home and I didn't have any money to buy food in Wolverhampton, so I always arrived home on Saturday evening ravenous and willing to eat anything. The only consolation I could take for this enforced abstinence was that it freed me from the need to go to the lavatory while at the match. The men's toilets were hideous examples of primitive squalor, worse than any brick privy in any back yard at the turn of the century. A faded painted notice on the bare brick announced the presence of the so-called convenience, but the suspicious stains on the walls near the gap in the wall that was the entrance, prompted the unwelcome question of what must the actual toilets be like if so many patrons preferred the outside wall? Perhaps mercifully, I never saw any toilets for women, so I was spared the unspeakable abominations that did duty as football's toilet arrangements for its devoted supporters.

Not that considerations of hygiene bothered me overmuch. I was too immersed in the excitement of it all. Nothing could compare to the thrilling journey from the station, past St Peter's church, set on a rise overlooking the market place, all the time feeling like a bottle of lemonade that has been violently shaken and is chock-full of delicious, tickly bubbles, just waiting to escape as the excitement spilled over. As I neared the ground there started to be signs of the forthcoming match: programme sellers, pocketing your threepence and handing over the precious gold and black programme. Then there were the other vendors, men with large placards, to which were pinned plastic star-shaped badges bearing photos of the players; on cup days there were the gold and black rosettes, sitting peaceably next to rosettes in the visiting club's colours, all with a crude replica of the FA Cup stuck in the middle. All round, mingling with the crowd were people selling team pictures, autograph sheets or little books, anything that would get the fans to part with 6d.

Then came the equally thrilling journey down the dingy narrow pathway at the side of the Molineux Hotel, which led to the turnstiles. Once through these, there was the vista from the top of the terraces of the South Bank, where the whole ground was laid out before me, the terraces filling up with expectant fans and the pitch a pristine green, just waiting for the sounds of "The happy Wanderer" to boom out from the tannoy system as a signal for the players to run out onto the field. I stood right at the front of the South Bank, by the wall that separated the terracing from the pitch, my place where I met the same people every week. There was the young married couple who followed Wolves home and away, the group of schoolboys from Wolverhampton Grammar School, who had to go to school on Saturday mornings and so turned up at the match in their school uniform, luckily yellow and black. There was a whole patchwork of familiar faces, interspersed with visiting supporters, with whom we shared our territory quite amicably.

For some football fans, supporting a team consists of taking a perverse pleasure in misery and disappointment, a constant expectation of disaster and doom, in which every win is accepted as an aberration that will soon pass, leaving only the expected defeat and derision. Not so with us Wolves supporters. We'd won the league in the 1953-4 season, been runners-up the following season and we had every hope for the 1955-6 season as well. After all, we'd scored 150 goals in the Championship winning season and 140 the following season and we had every expectation that Hancocks, Broadbent, Swinbourne, Wilshaw and Mullen would carry on where they'd left off at the end of last season. Scoring goals was what football was all about, for the system was geared to it. We confidently expected success, for hadn't Swinbourne scored 24 goals in the Championship season, Wilshaw had scored 25 and the wingers had scored more than 30 between them. We were, we repeated smugly to ourselves, no one-man team!

In fact, the 1955-6 season started just as we'd expected, with a glut of goals. First we hammered Manchester City 7-2 in August, which had the football writers searching for their superlatives. Maurice Smith began his report on the match, "Wonderful, wonderful Wolverhampton. Incredible, spellbinding Wolverhampton … this was wizardry, this was genius," with which understated assessment we agreed wholeheartedly! Of course, it couldn't all be unalloyed joy and some away matches were lost, to big teams such as Blackpool, Bolton and Manchester United, who, come the end of the season, were to top the table. But we never expected to lose at home: defeat on our own territory was unthinkable. It goes without saying that our local rivals, Birmingham, Villa and West Brom had to be defeated,

and we did it in style, beating Birmingham 1-0, with Ron Flowers injured and limping on the wing, and West Brom 3-2, with a team missing Billy Wright, Roy Swinbourne, Dennis Wilshaw and Bill Slater.

But, of course, overweening pride comes before a fall, and in November, while playing away at Luton, Roy Swinbourne was injured when he ran off the pitch and collided with a group of cameramen, who were sitting close to the touchline. It was to prove a fateful injury, for he never played seriously again.

Roy Swinbourne

That we lost 5-1 was of little importance, given that disaster. That his replacement, Jim Murray, was to prove an admirable successor was of little consolation to us: it was a bitter blow to take, and one not made any easier by losing at home 2-0 to Cardiff, a team which we'd beaten 9-1 on their own ground just a few weeks before, with Swinbourne scoring a hat-trick. Tempers were not improved by our losing in the third round of the cup to the old enemy, West Brom, in front of a crowd of 55,000.

For me, the only thing that rendered any defeat in the slightest bit palatable was the chance I got to see the stars play. When we lost to Cardiff we had Gerry Hitchens (soon to be one of the first soccer exiles to Italy), the pugnacious Trevor Ford and the famous Welsh fullback, Alf Sherwood, and when we lost to Blackpool 3-2 in January, we had the spectacle of Billy Wright, moved to fullback for the occasion, being given the runaround by the great Stanley Matthews, a runaround such as he probably couldn't remember happening to him before. When, in February, we lost 2-0 to the future champions, Manchester United, I got to see the famous Busby Babes, Duncan Edwards, Tommy Taylor, Roger Byrne and the like, all to perish too soon in the Munich disaster. There was always some great star to see: even the humblest First Division side had their star player – Blackpool had Matthews, Preston had Finney, Bolton had Lofthouse, Newcastle had Milburn and we were not afraid to show our appreciation of their skills. There was no booing, no abuse, but then winning wasn't everything in those more innocent days. In fact, even the match programmes gave credit where credit was due. In September 1955, the programme described the away match at Blackpool, the week before, which Blackpool had won, commenting on the superb form of Stan Matthews, who had won the game for Blackpool, as being not only "a treat for the crowd" but also saying, "we are not so insular as to be unable still to admire the Matthews technique, even though it may sometimes be embarrassing", concluding that Wolves were glad to have helped provide such good entertainment. No shades of the tribal wars that were to break out in the game before long.

With all the heart-stopping heroes that came to Molineux, it's no wonder that my great passion was autograph hunting. After every

FOOTBALL LEAGUE — FIRST DIVISION

MOLINEUX GROUNDS, WOLVERHAMPTON
(Covered Accommodation for 30,000)

SATURDAY, FEBRUARY 18th, 1956

Match No. 30   Kick-off 3 p.m.

Shirts: Gold   **WOLVES**   Knickers: Black

RIGHT   *SIMS*   LEFT

~~WILLIAMS~~

STUART   SHORTHOUSE
2   3

FLOWERS   WRIGHT   CLAMP
4   5   6

HANCOCKS   BROADBENT   MURRAY   BOOTH   WILSHAW
7   8   9   10   11

Linesman—Yellow Flag   Referee—   Linesman—Red Flag
J. C. MEREDITH   L. RICHARDSON   W. D. D. MADDOCKS
(Shrewsbury)   (Doncaster)   (Derby)

PEGG   VIOLLET   TAYLOR   WHELAN   BERRY
11   10   9   8   7

EDWARDS   JONES   COLMAN
6   5   4

BYRNE   GREAVES
3   2

WOOD

LEFT   RIGHT

Shirts: Red   **MANCHESTER UNITED**   Knickers: White

THE TEAMS ARE SUBJECT TO ALTERATION

The famous Busby Babes

home match I haunted the players' car park, waiting to waylay them as they came to collect their cars. The top players, badly paid as they were, generally managed to own a car, good, solid, dreary Austin Cambridges, or the family Morris, and I wrote in the back of my autograph book the registration numbers of the players' cars, so that I would know just which of them were likely to appear and be forced to give me their autograph. When they emerged from the players' entrance, they looked as unremarkable as any respectable young man; only the fans saw the invisible aura of heroism about them. They were dressed in ordinary sports jackets, blazers, flannels, with neat shirt and tie, just like any other lad of the time. There was no designer gear, no outlandish fashions – these would come much later.

I prowled about the car park, keeping a weather eye open for any players, waiting in line for autographs and the chance to get a word with my heroes. I treasured everything they said, repeating to my distinctly unimpressed school-friends such gems of information as, "Jim Mullen thinks they ought to have beaten Bolton", or, "Peter Broadbent thought their second goal was definitely offside". Once, by some great stroke of fortune, I managed to get the autograph of the great Jackie Milburn, and was proudly showing it off to other fans on the train home, when some foolish woman, ignorant beyond belief, enquired naively, "Who's Jackie Milburn?" leaving us all in stupefied silence.

Jackie Milburn plus autograph

I carried my autograph book everywhere, even on the bus to school, in case any of the Birmingham players should get on, and any mention of a personal appearance by players, where autographs would be available, had me going off to town to wait in yet another queue. Of course, I waited longest and most patiently for Billy Wright, always hoping he'd take notice of me, even though with my bird's nest hair and rag-bag clothes there was small chance of that. I treasured every word he said to me, wrote them all down in code in my diary, (and if I sometimes forgot the code and couldn't decipher them, it didn't really matter – they were indelibly etched in my memory, anyway), and I made my plans to play football for England and to marry Billy Wright one day (though not necessarily in that order). I chatted to Jim Mullen about games, about a young sixteen year old goalkeeper, Joe Dean, who had made his debut for Bolton on a freezing day, letting in four goals, one of which happened when he tried to punch the ball, which skidded off his gloves into the net. Jim Mullen showed great sympathy for the lad, but then, he had played in a cup semi-final when only sixteen himself, so I supposed he knew what it felt like.

The signed picture!

So obsessed did I become about autograph hunting that when my cousin came by a handsome signed photo of Tom Finney in full glorious colour, I was eaten up with jealousy, and when no amount of bribery or coercion could make him part with it, I despatched a photo of Stan Matthews to Blackpool, for the great man to sign it. When it came back, suitably inscribed, and was installed in prime position on my bedroom wall, honour was somewhat mollified and, although the ink has now faded so far as to be illegible, and the picture is darkened with age, it's still a trophy to treasure. I wonder what happened to the Tom Finney picture?

But, of course, autograph hunting was merely an adjunct to the serious business of matches and we had some fine diversions in the shape of glamorous matches with exotic foreign sides. In the middle of a miserable January we livened up the winter with a match against a South American side, San Lorenzo, whom we beat 5-1. How I managed to get there for a mid-week match is a story in itself: it came from an amazing stroke of luck. My Gran, who had struggled to keep her house going after my Grandad's death, hit upon the idea of letting out her front parlour and front bedroom to the daughter of her half-sister and her husband, who were looking for somewhere to live. This brought me into contact with Bill, the husband, who, like the Almighty, was to prove to be to me "a very present help in trouble", for he was a football fan and, not only did he have a television set upon which I could watch matches with him, but he was also blessed with a most benevolent disposition that led him not only to take me to football matches in his car, but also to pay my entrance fee to the matches. As far as I could see, it was an arrangement made in heaven, for when I was there, watching football with Bill, his wife would take herself over the road to take tea with her mother, leaving us to commune with football in peace and comfort. She very goodnaturedly accepted his enforced absences from home, taking me to matches at some ground or other, unable to fight against the power of sheer fanaticism. No doubt there was family gossip about this unorthodox arrangement, much tut-tutting, knowing glances and doleful prognostications that "It'll all end in tears," but I remained determinedly unaware of them. As far as I was concerned there was room in my heart for only football and Billy Wright, and, in any case, I had worse troubles to bother me.

If you are a girl football fan, horribly conspicuous by your rarity, then you are looked on as fair game, not only by the bum-grabbing pests who infest every large crowd but also by every callow youth, doomed to remain unnoticed by any girl of any discernment, who can use as his excuse for accosting you in a public place your shared interest in the team, and who feels emboldened to engage you in conversation about the match you've just seen, as a prelude to more tiresome antics. I met one such on the station one Saturday afternoon, while waiting for my train to Birmingham. As his opening gambit, true to form, he made some trite remark about the match, following this with a detailed narration of his past life, including his claim to have won the Military Medal in the Korean War at the beginning of the fifties. Granted, scrawny, seven-stone weaklings don't all have sand kicked in their faces by the hunk in the Charles Atlas advert, and the most unprepossessing people are capable of the most astonishing feats of heroism, but in this case, I very much doubted it. My distinct lack of enthusiasm for his company didn't, unfortunately, deter him and I was forced to spend the whole of the journey home in his importunate company. Out of sheer desperation, when he told me he came from Coventry, from what I thought was a safe distance, I gave him my address and he promised to write to me. We weren't on the phone, so I fondly believed I was safe.

However, worse was to follow. The next day was awash with torrential rain, which kept us all in the house for most of the day. In the late afternoon there came a knock at the front door, a most unusual occurrence, for all habitual callers came round the back to the kitchen door. To my horror, I opened the door to find on the doorstep, much resembling a half-drowned rat, sodden clothing clinging to his weedy frame, bicycle clips dripping rivulets, my importunate swain from the day before, having ridden over from Coventry on his bike in a veritable monsoon. Common courtesy demanded he be asked in, his sopping clothes dried in front of the fire and a warming cup of tea be provided, but, these tasks completed, conversation languished. The situation was only relieved by my dad coming in from work and offering to drive the lad, bike and all, back to Coventry in his car. I was mortified. Dad never took us in the car, so to take a stranger all the way to Coventry was a concession of the highest order. Thankful as I was for the deliverance, I felt awkward and embarrassed at putting my father to such trouble, but I was nevertheless heartily glad to see the car disappear up the road. However, undeterred by this less than perfect experience, my foolish admirer hung on for a while, writing me letters, until I went away to university and the acquaintance withered.

In spite of such unwelcome distractions from the serious business of football, however, the season wore on. The end of the season, which I always dreaded, for it brought the long desert of football-free months with it, came. Johnny Hancocks, having scored 168 goals in 378 appearances for Wolves, came to the end of his prolific career, being replaced the following season by Harry Hooper, signed from West Ham and promising great things. As for me, it had been a season of near bliss. True, I was as yet no nearer either to playing for England or marrying Billy Wright, but I really felt I belonged somewhere at last. Local people ribbed me goodnaturedly about my team, calling them "your Wolves". "How are your Wolves going to get on today?" they would ask and crow over the fact that "Your Billy Wright isn't playing today." The local newsagent saved me cut-price books on football and at last I had an outlet for all the passion and commitment that nobody else seemed to want.

Nowadays, when I see grown men (and women), wearing their team's shirt, openly weeping, tears coursing down their cheeks at some defeat in a vital match, when I feel the strength of the solidarity between the people of the Kop, experience the shared emotions of the fans – the lighter moments such as when one end of Anfield couldn't see who'd scored the goal because of the thick fog, and set up a chorus of "Who scored the goal?" only to be answered immediately by the chant of the player's name from the other end of the ground, whereupon a huge spontaneous chorus of "Thank you very much for the information" came back, as if they'd been rehearsing it for weeks – I feel a real glow of fellow feeling. For them, like me, the week is one of deprivation, neglect, the desperation of trying to make ends meet and salvage a little human dignity, but the weekend is something else again. Then, you become an infintessimal part of the legend, of the glory that is your team: you belong to it and you are entitled to bask in its reflected glory, which gives you the courage to get through next week.

The 1956-7 season

The beginning of the 1956-7 season brought a change. I was obliged to give up taking the bell and rattle to matches. Not only were they confoundedly inconvenient to cart about town both before and after the match, but we'd had a few near disasters with them, when the emotion of the moment had led to injudicious twirling of the rattle and over-vigorous clanging of the bell. Being struck unexpectedly from behind by a large wooden rattle was tantamount to being poleaxed by a shillelagh and to be smitten by a heavy metal bell, not to mention the clapper, was likely to reduce the most nice-natured fan to rage, so, reluctantly, I decided to forego them, in the interests of keeping enough supporters conscious long enough to watch the match. Mind you, it seemed that such advertisements of one's allegiance were still in vogue, for it was about this time that the school bell disappeared, leaving us for several days to change lessons at the whim of the teachers. It had, so the story went, been purloined one Friday afternoon, painted blue and white and taken to a Birmingham City away match, being abandoned in a convenient canal on the journey home, where, I suppose, it lies to this day, buried in sediment and shedding rust with every ripple.

What we needed, of course, was some less dangerous and more legitimate ways of advertising our devotion to our team. In these days of marketing men, all eager to screw the last penny out of supporters for replica strips (sometimes several in the same season), along with every other item that can be possibly personalised with the club logo: mugs, tracksuits, sweatshirts, miniature footballs, and the like, which have become the bane of every football supporting parent, it must be difficult to envisage a time when nothing was available, but we searched in vain. We even toyed with the idea once of scouring junk shops on the off-chance of finding a stuffed fox (on the understanding that there wasn't a chance in hell of ever finding a stuffed wolf), dressing it in Wolves strip and taking it to matches. But not only did we live in fear of some zoologically aware busybody accusing us of trying to pass off a fox as a wolf, but, in any case, even a moth-eaten old stuffed fox was nowhere to be found.

All I did find was a small pennant, (yet again a pale, unsuitable yellow), bearing the Wolves name on it in black, and made out of a thick, stiff felt material that couldn't possibly have fluttered in any breeze; it was so thick that even a force 10 gale wouldn't have been able to make it stir. Undaunted, I attached its ugly metal stick to the handlebars of my bike, to advertise my allegiance. Then, one fateful day, I was toiling up a steep hill on my bike, when I inadvertently touched the kerb with my front wheel, which spilled me into the road and smashed the bike against the sharp edge of the kerb, which snapped my pennant straight off, leaving it a muddy, sodden mess in the gutter, and a lethal-looking sharp spike sticking up from the handlebars. Afraid of having the dangerous spike poke me in the left nostril as I bent over the handlebars while negotiating some other steep gradient, I was forced to consign the whole sorry mess to the dustbin and abandon my search for the sort of goodies which, forty years on, are foisted upon us by the barrowload.

However, the 1956-7 season was famous for two notable events, one dire in its awfulness, the other wonderful. Good things first – I became the ecstatic owner of my first (and only) pair of football boots. At the beginning of the season my cousin, (he of the Tom Finney picture), was bought his first pair of football boots (though, in my recollection, he rarely played, though he did do what was seen as his duty in later life by supporting Birmingham, even going to away matches with them). This created in me such a ferment of envy that I immediately determined that, at the very least, I had to have a go with them. By some quirk of benevolent fate, he took the same size shoe as me (he being a few years younger), so we went over the field at the back of Gran's house and Buster was cajoled or coerced into letting me wear his precious new boots for a while. There he sat, hunched up, trying to make himself as inconspicuous as possible in case any of his mates should pass and see his mortifying condition, wearing my girls' shoes, while I cantered about over the grass, feeling for the first time the sensation of studs on grass, hearing the satisfying sound as leather hits leather and savouring the pleasure of being able to kick the ball prodigious distances. It was only my cousin's plaintive threat to tell his Mom if I didn't give him his present back that finally persuaded me, with a reluctant sigh, to unlace them, hand them over and return to my girl's shoes. In my heart, however, had just been made the implacable resolution to own a pair of my own.

The chance came quicker than expected. I went back to school in September and resumed playing hockey in my usual desultory manner. One afternoon, when I was involved in some dreary tussle with another form, I made for the ball, only to see, too late, a huge, thirteen stone virago from the Upper Sixth, stick waving menacingly, and a frightening expression of total concentration on her face, bearing down on the ball and on a direct collision course with me. She reached the ball a fraction before me and clouted it with deadly intent straight at me, striking me what I feared was a mortal blow on the left shin, just where the leg joined the foot. Gravely wounded, I limped off, too injured to take any further part in the contest. When I got home, this dreadful injury was paraded before my mother, (after all it had incapacitated me for all of half an hour), and, looking at the egg-sized swelling, she was surprisingly sympathetic. Seeing my chance, I argued plausibly that if I had leather football boots, which came up right over the ankle, instead of flimsy canvas pumps, I would not suffer such a wound again. I feared my arguments would be shot down in flames by Mom, who generally clung to her cash as does a limpet to a rock, but this time, to my joy, she fell for it and promptly took me down to the little local shoe shop, to see if she could inveigle the shopkeeper into parting with a pair of football boots cheaply. She was a formidable woman, my mother, an irresistible force in an old-fashioned, cross-over, flowered pinny and, although the shopkeeper was, as Mom said, "Too mean to give a blind man a light", he was no match for her steamroller technique and almost before I knew it, he'd parted with the goods and I was the proud owner of a pair of boots, fitting high over the ankle, and made from leather every bit as tough and unyielding as iron, and which had to be tamed by the assiduous application of veritable vat-loads of dubbin. We were never rich enough in our house to eat steak, but if we ever had, I bet it would have been just like those boots, as palatable as a live buffalo and just as hard to get your fork into. So hard were they that, once encased in them by means of mile-long laces, your ankles couldn't move at all, and to try to turn suddenly was likely to leave your feet facing one way while you faced another. But I was unrestrainedly delighted. Every evening I held the ritual of applying copious amounts of dubbin, rubbing it into the leather with loving care, if appreciably little effect. I took them to school on games afternoons, was thought quite barmy by the girls, but managed to get a little football practice with the lads, more than slightly impressed by a girl who had her own boots.

I also found another use for the dubbin. I discovered that if I rubbed it onto my school shoes it gave them the sort of shine usually only obtainable by the expending of much elbow grease. I was always in trouble at school for my scruffy appearance, so I thought that if my shoes, at least, were shiny, it would cover up a multitude of sins and get the Senior Mistress off my back. Unfortunately, dubbin, just smeared over the shoes, was just like Vaseline, sticky and attractive during the course of the day to dust, biscuit crumbs, dead insects, wet leaves and gravel, and I finished every day with the shoes looking like a sticky fly paper, with numerous gruesome corpses adhering to them. Unfazed by this, I scraped away the detritus of the day every evening and applied new dubbin when I was nurturing my precious football boots.

But all the time I was revelling in my new-found fortune, Fate was storing up a disaster of the first rank to torment me with – Wolves lost to Bournemouth in the Cup. On a freezing day in January, Wolves had met Swansea in the Third Round at Molineux and what a treat it had turned out to be! Swansea not only had another of the famous Charles family playing for them, this time Mervyn, but also the Welsh wizards Cliff Jones and the Allchurch brothers, Len and Ivor, who made a nonsense of the treacherous, icy pitch, gliding over it effortlessly and giving us all a football lesson. They were terrific, and it wasn't until Jim Mullen scored in the last minute that Wolves

Ivor Allchurch   *Cliff Jones*

managed to make the scoreline a respectable 5-3. With such a wonderful performance from both teams we went into the Fourth Round tie, a home match with lowly Bournemouth, with the idea that it was all going to be a breeze. We'd had some new players drafted into the side: Gerry Harris had replaced Bill Shorthouse, who'd retired, and Joe Bonson was filling Jim Murray's shoes, but the old half back line of Slater, Wright and Flowers, all England internationals, and the exciting Harry Hooper, who'd replaced Johnny Hancocks on the right wing, left no iota of doubt in our minds that it was going to be a doddle. It never entered our heads that we could lose. Before the match we exchanged banter and football programmes with the Bournemouth supporters and waited for the expected massacre of the innocents that was to come.

Once the match started, however, it didn't run according to the script at all. First, one of the goalpost fell down, struck by a player running into it at full tilt and there was a lengthy delay while little men in overalls ran about, carrying hammers, posts, buckets and sundry appurtenances of maintenance men, while the players watched, hardly able to keep a grin off their faces. This charade duly over, Bournemouth did everything to stop Wolves scoring. The rest, as they say in the movies, is history. Bournemouth won 1-0. The programme for the next match might have trotted out all the cliches about "It's all in the game" and "just one of those things", but we knew better. It was an unmitigated disaster and one we knew we'd never live down, and we all crawled home with our tails between our legs. I toyed with the idea on the way home of hurling myself dramatically into the canal, where I hoped I would float rather fetchingly like a latter-day Ophelia, before sinking romantically beneath the waves, killed by the Wolves' iniquity. But I didn't, reasoning, quite sensibly, that I'd be more likely to die of the scum and muck that floated on the surface of the water than from decent drowning. Even so, when, that evening, on the radio news, I heard the announcer, in his clipped formal BBC tones announce that the Bournemouth supporters had made a cake for their victorious team, iced on top with the message "Up the Cherries!" I hadn't yet regained enough of my sense of humour to laugh at the incongruity of the posh voice and the iced message.

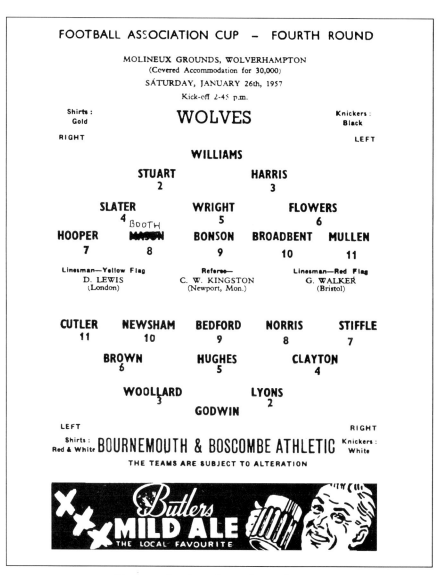

FOOTBALL ASSOCIATION CUP — FOURTH ROUND

MOLINEUX GROUNDS, WOLVERHAMPTON
(Covered Accommodation for 30,000)
SÁTURDAY, JANUARY 26th, 1957
Kick-off 2-45 p.m.

Shirts :
Gold

WOLVES

Knickers :
Black

RIGHT   LEFT

WILLIAMS

STUART   HARRIS
2   3

SLATER   WRIGHT   FLOWERS
4   5   6
BOOTH
HOOPER   MASON   BONSON   BROADBENT   MULLEN
7   8   9   10   11

Linesman—Yellow Flag   Referee—   Linesman—Red Flag
D. LEWIS   C. W. KINGSTON   G. WALKER
(London)   (Newport, Mon.)   (Bristol)

CUTLER   NEWSHAM   BEDFORD   NORRIS   STIFFLE
11   10   9   8   7

BROWN   HUGHES   CLAYTON
6   5   4

WOOLLARD   LYONS
3   2
GODWIN

LEFT   RIGHT

Shirts :
Red & White **BOURNEMOUTH & BOSCOMBE ATHLETIC** Knickers :
White
THE TEAMS ARE SUBJECT TO ALTERATION

The team that beat the mighty Wolves 1- 0

But it wasn't all gloom, of course. In spite of the natural pessimism of so many football supporters, let down too often not to expect the worst, we had a good season, wrestling as usual with Manchester United and finishing sixth in the league, behind them yet again. At the beginning of the season we started where we'd left off the season before, with a hatful of goals. In the first match we whacked Manchester City 5-1, before a crowd of 43,000, deeplying Don Revie notwithstanding, which feat had newspaper reporter Scott Hall waxing all lyrical. He called in "a dazzling, out-of-this-world show. A show fit to be flashed out on television, Eurovision, the lot, for the world's delight." We merely allowed ourselves a smug smile. We saw this stuff every week and we almost expected Jim Murray to score four goals every match.

When top of the table Luton came to Molineux next, of course we expected goals, but not the hatful we got. After seven minutes a latecomer, asking the score, was shattered to hear that we were already two goals down. However, by a quarter of an hour sanity was restored and we were level. You didn't dare take your eyes off the action for fear of missing something and when eight goals were scored in the first half, five to Wolves and three to Luton, I began to lose count. The pace never slackened in the second half, although there was only one more goal (to Luton) and Wolves won 5-4. A crowd of 46,000 had seen a pulsating match, and it was no wonder, after that display, that we believed that we were invincible. But it is a truism that the only thing worse than the fickleness of football fans is the hypocrisy of the Fleet Street hacks, and, to our rage, the London press began to write scurrilous stories about our heroes. Wolves had followed a 6-0 beating of Portsmouth with a 3-3 draw with Chelsea in the next match. This latter result produced an extraordinary outburst in the London press, who affected to cry crocodile tears and wring their hands over what they said was the poor state of the Wolves' defence, even having the nerve to suggest that it was so bad that they ran the risk of ending Billy Wright's England career prematurely because of the strain of being in a poor defence and having "to cover for the deficiencies of others". We were spitting mad. What had got up the noses of the London press was that Wolves, the fittest team in the league, who often scored two or three goals towards the end of matches, had pulled back a three goal deficit against Chelsea in the last thirteen minutes and thus had rescued a draw. How dare a provincial side draw with Ted Drake's wonderful Chelsea, they seemed to be saying, as if to suggest that there were no good teams north of the capital.

What a moment to savour, then, when, just three matches later, we humiliated the Arsenal 5-2, with our new young player, Colin Booth, scoring four of the goals. It was all the more satisfying to us to know that Stan Cullis had snatched Booth from under the nose of Matt Busby, when the lad was only 17. Dennis Wilshaw spent much of the game hobbling on the wing, but we only needed ten men to vanquish Arsenal. The press verdict was "A great game." It certainly was, and when we repeated our Houdini act and came back from three goals down with twenty minutes to go to win 4-3 against Preston, we began to believe that the Molineux floodlights were a lucky charm for us – we'd never lost under floodlights at Molineux. In spite of the triumphs, however, it wasn't to be the best season for us, for we finished sixteen points behind Manchester United. We had done our duty by beating our local rivals, which was some consolation, however. We beat Birmingham at home 3-0, West Brom 5-2 and won 3-0 at home to the Villa, although we lost to them 4-0 away.

If we were honest, though, we weren't satisfied. We'd lost out, yet again, to Manchester United, and having Alan Hoby write in the newspaper that we were "the Manchester United of the Midlands" infuriated us enough to swear eternal enmity to United and determine to have them dubbed "the Wolves of the North". There was, at this time, a popular calypso song about United, which went;

"Manchester, Manchester United,
A bunch of bouncing Busby Babes;
They deserve to be knighted."
which we always changed to
"They deserve to be blighted".

Ironically, it wasn't to be long before they were, which left us to sail unchallenged to the championship.

At this time Wolves were still the unchallenged kings of floodlight football and kept up the tradition of staging evening matches against foreign opposition. October saw the arrival of CCA from Rumania, their army team, and with a fine reputation. They'd played other English teams and been unbeaten but at Molineux they lost 5-1 and my friend Bill and I went home happy. Incidentally, in these days when European competition is commonplace, it's interesting to see that in 1956, in a newspaper article, Billy Wright was worrying that too many European matches might ultimately kill the public's interest. He voiced the fear that "after a couple of seasons, when the glitter has worn off a little" the crowds would be bound to fall off. I'm not sure whether it's comforting or irritating to find the same problems haunting the game for years on end, but it's interesting to see that even in the infancy of European competition doubts were being expressed about its long-term future.

Not satisfied with dragging Bill over to Molineux for the game with CCA, I next got him to take me to St Andrews to see the English 'B' team take on the Scotland 'B' team. 'B' internationals, where reserves were tried out before elevation to the national side, were a great feature then and enabled provincial supporters to see many promising players playing together in the same team, giving a preview, so to speak, of the next generation of international players. There was a lot of local interest in the game for Trevor Smith of Birmingham was playing for England, as were Don Howe of West Brom, and the man I'd come along to cheer, Harry Hooper of Wolves. Hooper, who'd cost Wolves a massive £25,000 when he'd

been signed from West Ham (the most any club had ever paid for a winger), oddly enough, was to shine like a comet for only one season and move to Birmingham in 1957, being replaced in the Wolves side by Norman Deeley. In the event, however, it wasn't Hooper who took the eye, but a young centre-forward, the sole representative of the Second Division, who played the match with a startling black eye and certainly took everybody else's eye – Brian Clough of Middlesbrough. He'd only made his debut for the club the season before but my dad and I, who didn't always agree on football matters, were at one with regard to this young man

Brian Clough of Middlesbrough

– he was a star of the future. Sadly, we were both wrong, for his career was to be cruelly cut short by injury and he had to turn his hand to management.

The end of the season brought to our attention, yet again, Manchester United, for they reached the Cup Final, where they came

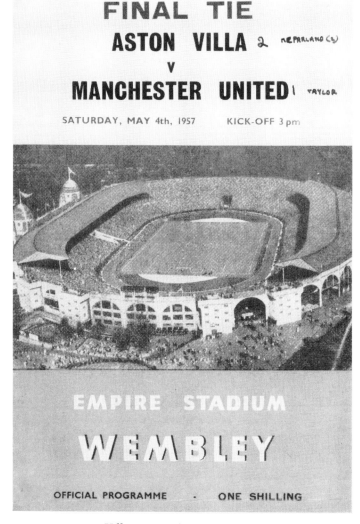

Villa capture the cup in 1957

up against Aston Villa. We Wolves fans didn't know what to do here: we hated them both. In the event we needn't have worried, for, although the Villa won, it was in the most controversial of circumstances, which left neither team satisfied. Peter McParland, in challenging (some said most unnecessarily) the United goalkeeper, Ray Wood, injured him so badly that he had to leave the field, leaving United, since no substitutes were allowed, without a goalkeeper. There had been all through the fifties discussions about allowing at least substitute goalkeepers, since so many showpiece finals had been over the years ruined as contests by injury to key players, but nothing was to come of the discussions for many years. Anyway, we had the pleasure of the Villa's triumph being tarnished by controversy and Manchester United actually losing a trophy, even if we did have to endure their insufferable air of injured innocence for months afterwards. What we didn't know then was that in 1962 the villain of the piece, Peter McParland, would actually become a Wolves player!

The final memory of 1956-7 also, in a way, belongs to Manchester United, for in December 1956 Molineux played host, for the first and last time, to a World Cup qualifying match. England played Denmark, winning 5-2, the goal scorers being Tommy Taylor, who scored 3 and Duncan Edwards, who scored the other 2, both of whom were Manchester United players. Roger Byrne, another of the Busby Babes was playing, along with the incomparable Stan Matthews on the right wing and the peerless Tom Finney on the

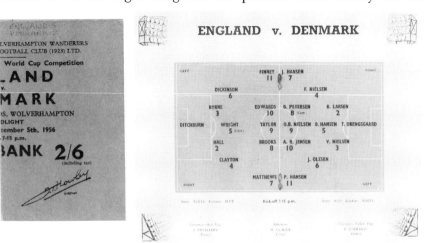

Busby Babes 5 Denmark 2

other. In spite of this star-studded team, the hypercritical Wolves fans set up the cry of "Bring on the Wolves!", but England won comfortably in the end, and I was thrilled to see all the stars in the same team, led, as usual, by our own Billy Wright. To add to this, the match was refereed by the famous French policeman Monsieur Guigue. For me, who never saw international matches, it was a real treat.

Although I couldn't get to watch England matches, with Billy Wright as its captain I naturally followed their progress closely, via the radio and newspapers. I cut out reports of their matches and stuck them in my scrapbook, along with action pictures of the matches. My interest in England had, I suppose, been first kindled by the sheer drama of the match in Vienna in 1952, when Nat Lofthouse earned the title of "The Lion of Vienna", and which raised

him to the level of a god in my eyes. Some time after, when he was playing for Bolton against Wolves, a frantic race for the ball with Billy Wright sent him hurtling off the pitch, over the wall and straight into my welcoming arms. I was sorely tempted not to give him back: here was a real, live hero, literally within my grasp. However, half a dozen willing hands grabbed him and thrust him back onto the pitch, back to the broadly grinning Billy Wright and on with the game.

His finest hour, though, had been that day in Vienna, a city full of British and Russian troops, a legacy of our little spat with Hitler seven years before. The atmosphere at the stadium was frenzied, for

Nat Lofthouse

national pride was at stake. The Russians, who were not very popular with their Austrian hosts, wanted England to win, and the thousands of British troops didn't dare even contemplate an English defeat, so the atmosphere was highly charged. And the match certainly lived up to its billing. The Austrians threw everything at the English defence, desperate to avenge their defeat in the war and when an Austrian player took an obvious dive in the penalty area and a weak ref gave a penalty, it seemed all over for England. Not so. At 2-2 Gil Merrick, in the England goal took the ball off a forward's head and in one movement threw it into the centre circle, where Finney passed it to Lofthouse. Then came the great 45 yard run for goal, hotly pursued by the Austrian defence, which ended, as all good fairytales do, with Lofthouse slipping the ball past the advancing goalkeeper into the net for the winning goal, only to collide with the goalkeeper and be knocked spark out, just as the ball hit the back of the net. What a win! The English soldiers were ecstatic: they said one victory on the football field was worth any amount of talking around a conference table, and from this moment football entered very firmly into the realms of international politics, not to mention high drama.

One thing that was not a presage of the future came in the fact that England pulled off famous wins against those teams that would come to dominate world football in the future, Germany and Brazil, beating Germany 3-1 in Berlin and Brazil 4-2 at Wembley. It was, really, just the calm before the storm, for the next decade was to see a decline in England as a major international force, at least until Alf Ramsey restored our pride by winning the World Cup in 1966.

New ideas were beginning to filter in, though. When the newspapers printed pictures of Albert Quixall taking ballet lessons from his wife, a ballet teacher, to help his flexibility and balance, die-hards snorted with disgust at what they saw as a descent into cissidom, but, after all, it wasn't that far removed from the fearsome Major Buckley of Wolves ordering the fourteen year old Billy Wright to take up ballroom dancing to help him learn how to change feet while moving quickly!

Albert Quixall tries a new training method

All too soon, however, the close season, enlivened only by international matches, was over, and we were back to the nitty-gritty of another season, with all its unanswered questions.

The 1957-8 season

When so many football fans seem to spend their days in a ferment of masochistic misery, aware that their players are nothing better than donkeys who couldn't get a job on Blackpool sands, it must be galling to think of an age and a team which inspired utter confidence, but such was the feeling as the new season started. After all, our players were all tried and tested, many of them were internationals and we'd known nothing but success for the last five seasons or so. This was to be my last season before I had to go away to university so I was looking for the team to serve up something special.

At the beginning of the season it looked like business as usual. The maximum wage was raised this year to £20 a week in the season and £17 a week in the summer, which, so it was calculated, should, with bonuses, allow a player in a reasonable First Division club to earn £1000 a year. It was assumed, of course, that players in the newly formed Third and Fourth Divisions wouldn't be paid anything like this maximum, or else their clubs would risk going out of business. How many players were on the minimum wage of £8 a week is anyone's guess. Signing-on bonuses were between £10 and £20, but players were allowed to ask for anything up to £300 if they were transferred at their club's request. Football, then, wasn't going to make players rich, and it certainly is no wonder that in later years, players who had given pleasure to millions, people like Wilf Mannion and Tommy Lawton, should fall on hard times. The change in footballers' fortunes since these times can best be seen in the fact that on the same day as a newspaper reported that Paul Gascoigne had just signed a sponsorship deal with a boot manufacturer at the age of 21, which would bring his earnings to £1 million, another paper reported that the late Jackie Milburn, recently deceased, had left an estate worth £70,000.

But there were, after all, some changes in the pipeline, with some clubs beginning to think of updating the facilities they offered at their grounds. They were beginning to be forced into some kind of change by competition from the cinema and from the new toy, television. Slowly, painfully slowly, football's monopoly over working-class entertainment was beginning to be questioned, and with post-war austerity now fading away, football clubs were facing increasing pressure to modernise their grounds and make watching football less of a trial of endurance. It didn't happen overnight, of course, but in 1958 the first cantilever stand was built (in Scunthorpe, of all places!), a type of stand that was to revolutionise the look of football stadia over the next few years. Not until the 1960s did clubs start to use modern building techniques, such as pre-cast concrete and aluminium sheeting, but these were used in Hillsborough in the early sixties. Actually, Port Vale had put forward plans to create "The Wembley of the North" in 1944, but they managed to complete only the tunnel and the paddock before the money ran out. Wolves' grandiose scheme in 1957 to create what was called "a Continental ground", came to nothing because the Council refused them planning permission, so, for the most part, the late fifties didn't really offer us a great deal more than we could have got just after the war.

People still queued for stewed tea at ramshackle refreshment counters, served from great, steaming urns, or mugs of Bovril, or, as the poet Phillip Larkin once wrote of Sheffield station "an awful pie". In fact, so little had changed about the quality of food on offer that in 1958 Nottingham Forest thought it necessary to put a disclaimer in their programme about the food sold at the ground, stating that the refreshment bars were "operated by private caterers, not the responsibility of the club". Truly, we didn't get much, but, then we didn't pay much either. Compared with today, when supporters are screwed out of money at every opportunity, football clubs in the fifties were not commercial enterprises at all. We certainly could never envisage a time when Newcastle supporters would be asked to pay money, just to give them a right to buy a season ticket; nor could we imagine the day when a callous Manchester United official would dismiss the fans by saying that if they can't get into Old Trafford to see the first team, they should come to watch the reserves or the youth team instead.

As for myself, the season brought little change. The word "teenager" had appeared from America, along with the distinctive modes of dress for the age's new elite: crew cut, DA or Tony Curtis haircuts for the boys, pony tails for the girls; Teddy Boy suits, draped lapels and drainpipe trews for the boys, multi layered full skirts with masses of petticoats for the girls, nipped in at the waist and worn with fluorescent bobby-sox and thick crepe-soled shoes. Not that I could rise to the heights of looking like an extra from the film "Rock around the clock", you understand. My style was definitely unfashionable grot. All I had was two choices: dress as young as possible and get into the boys' entrance for 9d, thus enabling me to take the bus all the way home, instead of having to walk part of the way, or try to look as old and sophisticated as possible in the hope that I'd meet Billy Wright and he'd notice me. In the end it was a compromise. I went in the boys' entrance at Birmingham for there was no-one there that I wanted to impress, and for Molineux I suffered hours of standing on uncomfortable, draughty terraces in high-heeled shoes and a tight skirt, most unsuitable wear for steep terracing, concrete walls and metal safety barriers, standing out in the open in all weathers, yet still pathetically determined to search for the elusive glamour I so conspicuously lacked.

How could I attain glamour? You know the old joke:

1st woman: "When I'm down in the dumps I buy a new hat."

2nd woman: "Oh, so that's where you get them from!"

Well, my clothes were like that. I was obliged to wear anything that my relatives bought for me, however unsuitable. For coats, for example, I was dependent on my Gran, whose choice of materials was eccentric, to say the least. First came a long, coarse-woven effort in large houndstooth check, orange and black, which did nothing for me but keep out the cold, and gave me appearance of a Belisha beacon. She followed that with a boxshaped number, in various shades of grey, with bold geometric patterns all over it, which stopped people in their tracks at twenty yards, and gave me the distinct appearance of wearing a patterned coffin. My hair, straight as rain in a monsoon, hid beneath my home-made knitted yellow and black bobble hat and for good measure I wore round my neck my Wolves scarf, embroidered with the names of the players.

How I wish now that we'd had today's unisex clothes, the ubiquitous jeans and Tee shirts, in which I might well have looked reasonably fetching as I had an excellent figure (thanks to all the football playing!) and tight jeans would have been the answer to a maiden's prayer, fulfilling both criteria of looking attractive while at the same time being eminently practical wear for standing on the terraces. But, then, girls did not wear trousers. Even in 1962, when I began teaching at an adult college, I was asked by the Head of Department to make it clear to the female students that they couldn't come to college wearing trousers.

At home as well, nothing had changed. We staggered through the week as usual, as near to destitution as made no odds, running out of essentials such as toilet paper, soap and tea, before the end of the week and pay-day. After a particularly spectacular bust-up between my parents we still walked the streets, Mom, me and the girls, until Dad had gone out and it was safe to return home and camp out in one of the bedrooms, only venturing downstairs when he was out at work or at the pub, until another truce was declared and normal life as we knew it could resume. I got out of the house as much as possible and dreamt of a new life, immersing myself in the cameraderie of football, where, for a few precious hours a week, I could dream I was somebody and meant something to somebody.

And for feeling you were somebody, Molineux was the place to be that season. At the start of the season things didn't look too special, for we won only two of the first five matches, but this did include beating the mighty Bolton 6-1 at home and Sunderland 5-0. When we played away to Everton a most unusual event occurred: there was a bottle-throwing incident that led journalist Bob Pennington to brand Liverpool as "the city with the worst record of football hooliganism", a view based mainly on some unsavoury incidents that had taken place the season before at Goodison, during a reserve match. So incensed was Mr Pennington that he advised the F.A. to tell the offenders, "one more rumpus and the ground will be closed". For those of us who have lived through the organised violence at football grounds of recent years, this would seem to be something of an over-reaction to what had been really only a minor incident, but it just shows what an alien phenomenon hooliganism was in those days. In truth, hooliganism had a long history, even then: my great uncle used to tell me horrifying tales of hooliganism at his favourite club, Millwall, that went back years, and it's a reputation that, even today, Millwall supporters guard jealously. There's a good story about trouble at Millwall as far back as 1947. Millwall were playing

Barnsley, and for some reason the Millwall crowd took a dislike to the referee and began to threaten violence. When the referee awarded Barnsley a penalty, the crowd's mood became so ugly that the Barnsley player deputed to take the kick actually toyed with the idea of missing it, so as not to inflame the crowd further. Then, thinking of the welcome £1 bonus he would get if he scored and they rescued a draw from the match he decided to score and risk the consequences!

My father also told blood-curdling stories of the violence and mayhem that regularly accompanied the Old Firm matches in Glasgow, of blood and gore everywhere and pitched battles on the terraces. He had once been present at one such confrontation and had been so terrified that he'd never gone back! But, of course, Glasgow wasn't England, and, considering the enormous crowds that attended football matches, any kind of crowd trouble was surprisingly rare.

Molineux certainly attracted enormous gates, for in the 1957-8 season, in a long unbeaten run of 18 games, we had gates averaging 33,000, with 55,000 turning up for the derby match against West Brom (which ended in a 1-1 draw). The personnel were beginning to change slightly, for Bert Williams had retired, to be replaced by Malcolm Finlayson, a crinkly-haired, quiet Scot, with none of Bertie's extrovert saves, but a solid performer nonetheless. Also, Harry Hooper's comet-like light, which had shone so brightly for a season, burnt itself out, and he left for Birmingham City, to be replaced by the impish Norman Deeley, who had once been the smallest boy to play for England schoolboys. Wolves seemed to go in for diminutive wingers with cannonball shots and a definite penchant for scoring goals. The great Johnny Hancocks, he of the net-bursting shot and permanent scowl, had been so small that (so the story went), when he sent off for a pair of football boots (size 4), the parcel came back addressed to MASTER J. Hancocks, containing not only the boots but also a free jigsaw puzzle! Deeley was a mighty atom in just the same mould, scoring 22 league goals that season.

To my delight, my team's exploits began to get the press as admiring of them as I was myself, and newspapers began to try to outdo each other in superlatives. When Birmingham were beaten

5-1 at St Andrews, the press talked of the Wolves' forward-line "tormenting ... this half slow, bewildered and demoralised defence", and when they beat Spurs 4-1 and Blackpool, Stan Matthews and all, 3-1, we just knew it was going to be our season. As every football fan knows, there is no taste sweeter than that of beating opponents that have been a thorn in your flesh for years, so when, at the end of September, we vanquished the mighty Busby Babes, we were in seventh heaven. By Christmas, Jim Murray, gawky and unprepossessing off the pitch, was beginning to look more and more like Roy Swinbourne on it, and had scored 16 goals. To our old goal-scorers of Broadbent, Wilshaw and Mullen, had been added Murray, Deeley, Colin Booth and Bobby Mason, all slotting seamlessly into the team as required and scoring goals galore.

This being my last season before I went away to university, I was determined to try to get to a few away matches if I could. It is a law of life that nothing is so irritating as people who stubbornly refuse to appreciate the importance of football and the paramount necessity of supporting your team through all the vicissitudes of life, so when my stingy relatives refused to cough up the required cash to enable me to follow my team away, I gnashed my teeth in silent rage and frustration. Finally, an appeal to my Gran's good nature, and a couple of bob from my brother, who was at work, raised the necessary cash for a trip to Manchester, to see Wolves play City. I'd never been to Manchester: (let's face it, I'd never been anywhere – I was as insular as a desert-island dweller), but one dull November day found us on the station at Wolverhampton, intending to take the football special to the match. Years of mindless vandalism on trains, reducing them to so much scrap iron, has left the idea of special football trains as nothing more than a dim, half remembered dream, but then, everybody went away by train, even the players. There were no luxurious coaches, with their video equipment and tables for playing cards. In those days it was just the same train as the fans travelled on. Of course, for us, that was half the attraction; we were to travel on the same train as our heroes!

As we waited on the wind-swept platform on a uniformly grey day, we suddenly caught sight of the players drifting onto the platform in twos and threes. To our intense delight, (so intense, indeed, that we were all but struck dumb by the singular honour), Jim Mullen caught sight of us and came over to thank us for coming so far to support the team. Only too gleefully aware of the envious glances the other kids were casting in our direction, we revelled in being singled out so obviously. If there ever was such a thing as street-cred in those more innocent days, then we would have had it just then!

To add to the euphoria, the match itself was real humdinger. We stood on the terraces with the friendly City supporters, who were puffed with pride when their team took a three goal lead with only twenty five minutes to go. We weren't worried, (or so we told them), for we were used to our team scoring several goals in the last minutes of a match. As if on cue, Wolves launched a furious onslaught on the City goal, scoring three times in eight minutes and finally running out winners 4-3. "We wuz robbed!" was the cry of the City supporters, but we, with an airy wave of the hand and a nonchanant "I told you so!" went on our way. While waiting for the train back, we said to Jim Mullen, "We didn't think you were going to do it", to which he replied, after carefully looking round to see who could hear him, "Don't tell Stan, but neither did we!" On the train going back I wished most fervently that I could afford to go away with the team every match, I'd so much enjoyed the experience. The Manchester people had been so friendly to us in the town before the match, the City supporters had been so good-humoured and made us so welcome, we'd rubbed shoulders with the players and, to add to all that, we'd won the match! As far as I was concerned, this was the life!

However, it seemed that the Almighty is not a Wolves fan, (though heaven knows why not!), for it was to be March before I raised enough money to go away with the team again, to the City Ground, Nottingham, to have the infinite pleasure of seeing the team win again, 4-1, and watch them steamrollering to the Championship, with Murray scoring 32 goals and the team as a whole scoring 116 times. It was a wonderful season, the only thing that took the gloss off it being the fact that we came so close to the League and Cup double, reaching the sixth round of the cup before losing to that old enemy, Bolton, 2-1, before a crowd of 56,000.

In the third round of the cup we'd been drawn away against Lincoln City, and I'd planned to go, since Jim Mullen had sent me tickets for the game. However, I was thwarted, as so many have been thwarted before and since, by the sheer ineptitude of British Rail, who held up my train from Birmingham to Wolverhampton in a smoky dark tunnel for so long that when it finally reached Wolverhampton, the football special to Lincoln had long since gone. I've never been one for howling, but I felt close to it then, standing on a freezing and unwelcoming station platform, watching the rails stretch out into the distance, and my train well out of sight. It was no use Jim Mullen, who had scored the winning goal in an unconvincing 1-0 victory, telling me it hadn't been a match worth seeing, a dour struggle on a half-frozen pitch which made good football impossible and keeping your feet very difficult: I'd so much wanted to be there. Consolation came in the next round but one, however, when I, along with 55,000 others, saw the team beat Darlington 6-1, after an equally emphatic win at home to Portsmouth in the previous round. Then came Bolton, and the League and Cup double dream was over.

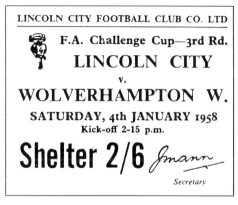

LINCOLN CITY FOOTBALL CLUB CO. LTD

F.A. Challenge Cup—3rd Rd.

LINCOLN CITY
v.
WOLVERHAMPTON W.

SATURDAY, 4th JANUARY 1958
Kick-off 2-15 p.m.

Shelter 2/6 *Jmann*

Secretary

Lincoln 0   Wolves 1

There were, however, con-solations. It's difficult to think now, when every football fan knows the great players of the world as well as he knows his own team, when a lot of them, indeed, are part of our teams, and when European competitions are for ever on our television screens, that in the 1950s only the biggest names were even known to us and to see such people in action in the flesh was a definite rarity. Wolves, the pioneers of floodlit friendlies, came up trumps again, and in October, the champions of Europe, Real Madrid, came to Molineux. It was a terrific game and we were able to feast our eyes on stars such as Di Stefano at centre forward, the wingers Gento and Matteos. In fact, virtually the whole team was made up of internationals. We were without Billy Wright, away on international duty, but we still won 3-2 and went home happy, convinced the old floodlight magic was still working.

The same season I went to St Andrews twice to see foreign opposition. First came Barcelona, in the old Inter-Cities Fairs Cup, whom Blues defeated 3-2, to go through to the final. Not long after this they played a friendly against Italian club Sampdoria, now a household name, thanks to television, but then just a name. We hardly knew where they came from, but they beat Blues 4-2 none-theless. At centre forward they had Eddie Firmani, who had recently left Charlton to play in his native Italy, one of the first in a trickle of players choosing to play abroad, a trickle that before much longer was to become a stream.

In spite of one of the most successful seasons in the team's history, which should have had us all on cloud nine, the 1957-8 season was irrevocably blighted by one word – Munich. February 6th 1958 is a date that is for ever etched in the memory of every football fan of my era, just as the name 'Hillsborough' sends a shiver down spines today. Manchester United had been in Belgrade, to play out a 3-3 draw with Red Star, Belgrade, in the European Championship, and had touched down, in atrocious weather, in Munich, for refuelling. On the takeoff, in freezing, snowy conditions, the plane had crashed on the runway, wiping out at a stroke most of the best English league team since the war, along with many journalists and back-room staff at the club.

I was at home that evening, crouching by the fire in the kitchen, trying to keep warm on a raw winter night, when my dad came in from work. His first words were,

"Isn't it terrible about Manchester United?"

I, who hadn't heard the news on the radio, thought he was referring to the match, which had, by all accounts, been rather rough. When I heard the news of the accident, my first reaction was one of disbelief. After all, we'd only just heard reports of the match, and they'd all been alive and well then. They just couldn't be dead so soon after. Of course, there was no mistake, and for the next few days, the whole nation, or so it seemed, was glued to the radio to hear the regular bulletins put out about the amount of dead and other casualties. During the war we'd been glued to the radio in just the same way: it had been our lifeline in the darkest days of the war. Now here it was being our death-line, for there seemed to be so many dead. So many young lives had been lost: Roger Byrne, Tommy

Taylor, whom I'd seem playing for England at Molineux; Geoff Bent, David Pegg (whose picture adorned my bedroom wall); Eddie Coleman, he of the pop-star charisma, Billy Whelan, Mark Jones – all dead. Even the great ex-England goalkeeper, Frank Swift, now a journalist, had perished: Swifty, that gentle giant who could pick up the ball with one giant hand like picking up an apple, and his genial smile, was gone. Billy Foulkes, Johnny Berry, Harry Gregg, Matt Busby, Duncan Edwards were all badly injured. Only Ray Wood and Bobby Charlton seemed to have got off lightly. Years of work wiped out in one moment of horror; years of promise that would not come to fruition. Some players, like Jackie Blanchflower, would never play football again. It was a disaster that was difficult to take in.

The ripples of the tragedy spread out far beyond Manchester. I hated United, they were our greatest rivals and so often pipped us for the championship, but I grieved for the senseless waste of so many young lives. My dad, who'd known Johnny Berry when he'd played for Birmingham, always asked after his health first when he came in from work and we all monitored the progress of the injured from the bulletins put out about them on the radio every day. Goalkeeper Ray Wood, injured in the crash, had a record played for his daughter on "Two Way Family Favourites" one Sunday lunchtime, which perked us all up a bit, but one morning, when my mother shouted me to get up for school she added, "Duncan Edwards has died. It's just been on the news on the wireless," and I shed tears for the young man who'd had the most talent of them all. Duncan Edwards, so the doctors said, only lingered a fortnight after the crash

Duncan Edwards,
Dudley's most famous sporting son

because he was so fit: it was scant consolation. He was only 21 and
had already played 18 times for England. It had once been a great
source of irritation to me that Matt Busby had been able to snap up
this local Dudley lad from under the very nose of the club he ought
to have played for; (Wolves, of course!), but to lose him this way was
unthinkable. We often hear Paul Gascoigne referred to as "the new
Duncan Edwards", but he isn't. He certainly has Edwards' talent, but
what he lacks is Edwards' temperament and character. Duncan
Edwards had a maturity both on and off the field beyond his years,
(something that no-one has ever been able to accuse Gazza of!) and
was a quiet, reflective, unassuming lad who liked the quiet peace of
fishing, which gave him time for reflection. If Gazza had been
blessed with his temperament he'd have been the eighth wonder of
the world.

When Duncan Edwards was buried in Dudley, his coffin was
carried by local players, Billy Wright, Don Howe, Pat Saward and
Peter McParland and by his England colleague Ronnie Clayton from
Blackburn and two of the new generation of United players, Gordon
Clayton and Bob English, and five thousand people lined the streets
of Dudley to pay their respects to the town's most famous son. Many
towns held services to pay tribute to the lost young men and I went
to one in Birmingham, at St John's church in Sparkhill, a service
attended by many local footballers. My friend and I walked up to the
church from the bus with Bryan Orritt and other players from the
Blues and all the other local teams turned out in force, with Billy
Wright reading the lesson. There is, of course, no room for partisanship in the face of such tragedy and I gave a full double-page spread
in my scrapbook to the disaster, adding my own epitaph, over-
dramatic perhaps, but sincerely felt:

"They lost the only game they didn't reckon on losing – the game
with death."

There have, of course, sadly, been many tragedies in football, and
many innocent people have lost their lives. In the Bolton disaster of
1946, for example, 33 people died and over 500 were injured. Ibrox
in 1971 saw 66 dead, and the Bradford fire of 1985 claimed 56 lives.
Most people remember the disgraceful scenes witnessed by millions
on television at the Heysal stadium, where 39 supporters were killed

and no-one will forget the scenes of carnage at Hillsborough in 1989. It is always impossible to find words on such occasions, but David Lacey of "The Guardian" summed up the feelings of everyone after the Bradford fire, writing:

"We talk about 'tragedy' when we mean 'disappointment' and 'disaster' when we mean 'defeat'. When real tragedy and disaster occur, we tend to be stuck for the right words."

He's right, of course: these things touch us all. And yet, it seems to me that Munich touched so many more people more deeply because it was the only football disaster in Britain where it was not the fans who were the victims, but the players. For the victims of Hillsborough, for example, we grieved for people we didn't know: at Munich we grieved for people we thought we did know, who had been part of our lives ever since we became football fans, and the effects sent a pall of suffering over all the country. Of course, these young men's lives were no more valuable than those of the lost fans: it just seemed to us fans more of a personal loss, somehow, and for the rest of the season we watched every week this patched-up, traumatised, rag-tag-and-bobtail team try to get through its remaining fixtures. They bought players from other teams to help them limp on until the wounds had had a bit of time to heal. They bought Stan Crowther from Villa, Ernie Taylor from Blackpool and, somehow, they got through the season. Of course, there were those only too keen to tell us that Wolves wouldn't have won the championship that year had it not been for Munich, but the Nottingham Forest programme of March 15 set us straight on that score.

"Even before the tragedy of Manchester United, Wolves had forged so far ahead with a big points margin that there seemed nothing ... to prevent the Staffordshire side winning the championship this season and so deprive Manchester United of a hat-trick of wins".

Be that as it may, you had to experience the huge wave of sympathy that followed United into every match they played for the rest of that season to see just how deeply the tragedy had touched football fans all over the country. It was something I've never experienced since.

Looking back with the benefit of hindsight on those days of

universal sympathy and admiration for a club that could rise from the icy runway of Munich airport to conquer the world, it strikes me that 1958 marked the beginning of the legend that is Manchester United today. After all, like the mythical Phoenix the club had risen from the ashes, led by the legendary Matt Busby, who himself had cheated death and lived to fulfil what must surely be a divine prophecy of greatness. What seemed to happen was the establishment in the minds of fans everywhere of the unshakable belief that United were the chosen of God, hand-picked by the Almighty to represent English football for at least the next 40 years. How else can you explain the po-faced reverence of today's commentators, whose voice falls to a hushed, respectful whisper whenever they speak of the team; the obsequious deference of interviewers, the rapt attention offered to the venerable Alex Ferguson's every cliché. It surely must be religious awe that leads John Motson to gasp breathlessly the name of each hero, as he receives the ball:

"Beckham! ..."

as if expecting, as a matter of course, some magical piece of skill to ensue from every touch of the chosen of the Gods.

And when the demi-god glides down the wing, poetry in motion, looks up in full flight and delivers an inch-perfect cross to the ball-boy behind the goal, before slipping over, ending on his bum in a patch of particularly cloying mud, greeted by the ecstatic hoots of derision from the opposing supporters, Mr Motson, an acolyte at the shrine of the immortal United merely murmurs:

"He'll be disappointed with that",

perhaps wondering whether "divinity" is quite the word, after all.

But, of course, all this was for the distant future, and meanwhile we had to get through the rest of the 1957-8 season. Wolves won the league title but there was a price to be paid for that precious success, a price personal to me, for during the summer, Billy Wright married. Of course, there had been speculation in the press for weeks before the event, for his bride was just as famous as he was: Joy Beverley, on of the famous Beverley Sisters singing group. She was a high-profile star in her own right, but when I heard the sick jokes about the relationship:

"Have you heard? Billy Wright's broken his leg."

"How did he do that?"
"Jumping for Joy!"
my misery was complete.

To football fans it was all a show-business event, with Billy Wright as only a bit-part player in it. As for me, I was glad that when the awful event finally came, I was on a camping holiday, only the second holiday I ever had with my parents, half drowning in a field on the road from Totnes to Paignton in Devon, trying to prevent the torrential rain from washing away our huge, army-surplus bell-tent, bought cheap by my dad, and probably once owned by Baden Powell himself, judging by its threadbare state. I lay at night on my damp, clammy rubber ground-sheet, the smell of the wet earth in my nostrils and the feel of unmentionable creepy-crawlies, come up from the wet earth beneath to join me under my blankets, and cried, which made the inside of the tent as wet as the outside. To the soggy morass of my ragged nerves and tortured emotions was added the quagmire of the campsite, as we trudged round for four days, up to our ankles in glutinous mud, digging trenches all round the tent, in a vain attempt to prevent an icy river from carving a path straight through it and washing us clean away, before common sense prevailed and we packed up our sodden canvas and soggy belongings and went home.

The 1958-9 season.

As every football fan knows, supporting a team, whether it is successful or not, is an exhausting business. If your team is successful you have to contend with envious sniping from rival fans, the application of discourteous epithets, both to yourself for supporting such a lucky, big-headed and soon-to-be-at-the-bottom-of-the-table where-they-belong team, and to your beloved team, whose players either suffer from indelicate diseases or some irregularity of parentage. If, on the other hand, your team is numbered amongst the vast army of also-rans, you are obliged to endure snorts of derision every time their name is mentioned, or unflattering comments about your players, generally comparisons to various members of the animal kingdom – donkey, great ape or carthorse being the most flattering. Indeed, to get through the season at all you need a vast amount of stamina, allied to the skin with the thickness of a rhinoceros hide.

Dennis Wilshaw gets the better of Blues' Trevor Smith

With the roller-coaster of emotional turmoil of the previous season came the need for a little calm and order for this one, although the cause was not helped by Dennis Wilshaw upping and leaving us for his local team, Stoke City. Considering he'd scored 117 goals in 232 games for us, it seemed he would leave a hole that would be difficult to fill. Actually, he was a bit of a rarity in football at that time, for he was an academic, a schoolmaster, who lived and worked in Stoke while playing for the Wolves. It was something of a rarity in those days for players not to be based in the town where they played, and yet, oddly enough, Wolves had two such players, for Bill Slater was also an academic who had played for the England amateur side before playing for the professional side. Both men stood out from their fellow players by dint of their cultured accents and obvious gentility. It was something of a novelty to see pictures of Dennis Wilshaw on the sports pages of the newspapers, clad in academic gown and clutching his books, rather than covering himself with mud and glory on the football pitch. Bill Slater, most cultured of wing-halves, wrote his thesis for his Master's degree, I remember, on some esoteric aspect of high jumping! Listening to radio interviews with these two men was a real experience, with their clear diction, impeccable grammar and never a "sick as a parrot" or an "over the moon" between them! In any case, Dennis Wilshaw had just scored four goals for England against Scotland at Wembley, when England won 7-2, so I felt he was going to leave a gaping hole in the team.

I was interested in their academic background, of course, because I was destined for university, a world about which I knew nothing at all. When I went up to Leicester University in October 1958, to study French, I hadn't a clue what to expect. In those days very few working-class girls went on to higher education, and, amongst the 800 students in the university in those days, I was probably the only working-class girl. Because I knew nothing about universities, how they worked and what they did, I chose which universities to apply to by the only criteria I knew. I applied to both Nottingham and Sheffield on the principle that they both had two football teams and I could watch players like Ron Springett, who played in goal for Wednesday, while Forest could offer me Stuart Imlach. What decided me, however, was that Leicester City had winger Derek Hogg playing for them, and I looked forward to seeing him play. Although I was offered a place at all three universities, then, I opted for Leicester, only to discover that no sooner had I accepted my place there than Derek Hogg was transferred to West Brom, where I could have best seen him play by staying at home! Still, Leicester it had to be.

It was, of course, the season when Wolves retained the championship, equalling the feats of Portsmouth (who had done it in the 1949 and 1950 seasons), and Manchester United (who'd done it in the 1956 and 1957 seasons). Unfortunately, I wasn't going to find it easy to be there to see the great triumph take shape. At university I was expected to spend my time discussing the poetry of Baudelaire or the philosophy of Descartes, rather than the skills of Jim Murray or the genius of Tom Finney. I found it all horribly foreign. I mixed with determinedly middle-class girls, called Celia, Helen or Angela, from cosy middle-class backgrounds and with cut-glass accents, to whom 'centre forward' or 'goalkeeper' conjured up visions of stirring encounters on the hockey field against the rival girls' school. Even the boys were not by any means all fanatical football fans, although I was lucky enough to find a fellow Wolves supporter, whose mother predated me as a fan by many years, for she had gone to every match for many years and even written a report on every match after the game.

If I couldn't go to every match while I was up at university, however, I still managed to fit in a fair few before I went up in

October. Things started well enough, with the glut of goals that we spoilt Wolves supporters had come to expect, winning the first match 5-1 against Nottingham Forest. However, three matches against the hated London clubs gave us only one point, and we'd lost to detestable Chelsea most mortifyingly, 6-2. In the Chelsea side that day, scoring five of his side's six goals was a precocious eighteen year old, Jimmy Greaves, soon to become a soccer legend. Watching him now on television, avuncular, slow of speech and seemingly of thought, it is difficult to believe just how lightning fast he was on the pitch. His speed of thought and movement were phenomenal and I lost count of the times I saw time hovering vaguely in the penalty area, seemingly offering no threat, only to strike cobra-like and grab yet another goal from not even a half-chance. Like Autolycus he was the archetypal "snapper-up of unconsidered trifles".

After the first ten matches of the season, we'd lost four and were in ninth place in the league, although we had done what we saw as our duty and beaten Villa 3-1 and 4-0. In October, however, we beat Manchester United 4-0, a post-Munich side, to be sure, but one which contained their new £45,000 signing, Albert Quixall, and on a day when we were without Wright and Broadbent, on duty for England, although United were without Bobby Charlton and Wilf McGuinness, also on international duty. Still, a win against United was still a win, and always to be rejoiced at.

After I went up to university in October the team got better, rattling in the goals. During the Christmas vacation I saw them whack Portsmouth 7-0, in spite of the efforts of the great Jimmy Dickinson, England wing-half. In the Portsmouth team that day, (and giving away a penalty, which, lucky for him, his goalkeeper, Norman Uprichard saved!) was Derek Dougan, showman and centre-forward, who, in the future, was to prove to be something of a saviour for Wolves. That day it was quite a sight; Derek Dougan, lanky, thin, long as a street, up against small, chunky Billy Wright, who had to jump a foot in the air to reach the top of Dougan's head! Naturally, the duel was won by Billy Wright! We were, by then, up and running, heading for the title. Losing 2-1 at home to Chelsea in January was a blow, to be sure, but we put six goals past Leeds and beat Arsenal 6-1, so honour was satisfied. In the last few matches we were unstoppable, beating West Brom 5-2, Luton 5-0 and Leicester 3-0. The team was an absolute pleasure to watch and that year we scored 110 goals and won the championship by six points from (as usual!) Manchester United.

Being away at university, in an alien environment, meant that not only was getting to matches difficult but it was all the more necessary, for I needed to keep in touch with my roots. I didn't miss home: that was at best awful and at worst unbearable, but I missed that feeling of belonging that I got in my own corner of Molineux, surrounded by the same people every week. Of course, I went to Filbert Street to watch Leicester (even minus Derek Hogg), first to see them play Borussia Dortmund, whose gold and black colours put me in mind of my precious Wolves. Their inspiring colours weren't enough, however, to ensure success, for Leicester beat them 2-1. It was misery, however, when I went to see them play Wolves, for I was horrified to see our strongest side beaten 1-0.

In the cup that year we were our usual indifferent selves. The season before we'd had an unusually good run, reaching the sixth round before going out, but this season saw us back to our usual woeful cup form. Beating Barrow in round three had been no trouble, but then in round four we were brought up against our bogey team, Bolton, who beat us 2-1. This match proved to be something of a first for me, for the crowd was 56,000, the atmosphere was terrific, and it was the first and only time I felt afraid in a football crowd. The crush of the crowd on the South Bank became so so great at one point, with the knots of fans swaying and pushing forward as the game became more exciting, that I became carried along by the irresistible force of a human tide, becoming crushed so closely up against a block of other human bodies that I could hardly breathe. Such was the pressure on my ribs that I waited, half suffocated, for the inevitable crack of bones giving way under the pressure. As I waited, with this awful feeling of helplessness, feeling as if I was drowning, suddenly, somewhere, someone moved fractionally, and I could breathe again. I'd had a narrow squeak, no mistake about that, and my ribs were bruised for weeks, in what had been my most terrifying experience in a football crowd. To compound the misery, we lost, and the cup was over for us for another year.

The cup wasn't quite over for me, however, for in March there was a cup semi-final replay one afternoon at St Andrews, Birmingham, between Luton Town and Norwich City, and I came down from Leicester to see it. Luton had Sid Owen playing for them, whom my dad had known when he played for Birmingham and Norwich had their famous stalwarts, Terry Bly and Len Ashman. Luton won, only to be beaten by Nottingham Forest in the final.

This season was something of a turning-point for me. Firstly, I was away from home, trying to fit into the alien environment of university, trying to fit in, to get on with people from completely different back-grounds from my own, while also being expected to solve the regularly recurring crises at home, all the while trying to keep some sort of personal identity that could so easy be submerged under the weight of all the expectations and demands put upon me. Up till then I'd hung on to an identity that was inextricably linked with the Wolves; but an era was coming to an end. Almost imperceptibly, the team I'd supported earlier in the decade was changing. Bert Williams and Bill Shorthouse had retired; Roy Swinbourne had been forced out by injury; Dennis Wilshaw had gone, and then, at the end of this season, I lost the two people from the team that I had always considered to be exclusively mine – Billy Wright and Jim Mullen, thus severing the links that had bound me so closely to the team. It was as if a light had gone out, and from then on, supporting the team always lacked that vital spark. A typical 'girlie' reaction, you might say, and I suppose you'd be right, in a way, for I'd certainly gained a lot of emotional comfort from watching the same players, playing in largely the same team every week, from my own vantage point on the terraces, feeling that I really belonged there and was part of the story that was the Wolves. On the other hand, there can be no need to apologise for regretting the passing of those players that had made the team great. After all, didn't their supporters feel bereft when Andy Cole left for Manchester United, or Gary Lineker joined Barcelona? Unless the team belongs to the supporters then the game is doomed. Anyway, Wolves were still my team, nothing could change that – it just wasn't the same team, that's all, and things were never quite the same again.

The 1959-60 season.

October 1959 saw me back at University, where I couldn't really afford to go to Wolverhampton very often, for even a full grant didn't stretch to much more than paying for my board and lodging, bus fares at twopence a time and a visit to film club once a week. I always arrived home for the vacation penniless, my last money having been spent on the bus fare back from Leicester to Birmingham. Then I found myself dependent upon my relations for sustenance until the next term began. Trips to Molineux generally had to be made before I went up in October, or, relations willing, during the other vacations.

Pity, really, for the 1959-60 season was to be the last really great season for my team, for the team of the great era, for it was during this year that we came closest to the cup and league double that had eluded us in the 1957-8 season, winning the cup and being runners-up in the league to Burnley. The race for the championship was a really pulsating affair, going right to the last match of the season. Wolves were still pulling in the crowds: in the 1958-9 season they'd averaged 38,000, topping 52,000 on two occasions, and during the following season, the cup winning season, a crowd of 56,000 saw them lose 3-1 to Spurs in April and, although they beat Chelsea after that, in front of 61,000 people, Burnley won rather luckily on the same day at Manchester City, and thus took the title.

As for me, shades of the future were already gathering around me, for the following year I was to spend the whole year away in France, so it was imperative that I store away as many memories as possible to last me while I was in exile. One of these was standing on the terraces with my future husband, watching my team; (he supported West Brom), beat Fulham 9-0. In the Fulham team were stars such as Graham Leggatt on the wing, George Cohen at full-back, Alan Mullery at wing-half, and a certain Jimmy Hill at inside forward, he of the

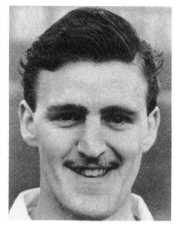

Jimmy Hill before the beard

chin to rival that of his Chairman, Tommy Trinder, a chin so pointed and sharp you could dig the ground with him. Perhaps it was this hammering at Wolves that decided him that his future lay elsewhere, for in only a couple of years he was to gain a measure of immortality as the man who helped to abolish the maximum wage for players and so change the game for ever.

Meanwhile, the breathless battle for the league went on, and the team, now without the influence of Billy Wright and Jim Mullen, for the first time since 1949 got to the Cup Final. Although I felt infinitely sad that both players had missed the triumph, it was totally satisfying to have beaten the hated Villa in the semi-final at the Hawthorns, home of our other deadly rivals, West Brom, thus rubbing it in that we were top dogs on our patch. The final itself, against Blackburn Rovers, was something of an anti-climax, being another of those finals ruined by injury. The Blackburn full-back, Dave Whelan, broke his leg just before half time and from then onwards the result was never in doubt. Blackburn's star players, Ronnie Clayton and Bryan Douglas, with a man short, were powerless to stop the Wolves, who ran out easy winners in the end, 3-0, but the victory was far from satisfactory. Once more the case for allowing substitutes seemed overwhelming. Not that we didn't shed tears of joy as the trophy was paraded around Wembley, resplendent in its black and gold ribbons, and I crowed over my dad for weeks afterwards, reminding him that when his Blues had gone to Wembley in 1956 they'd lost. But, to be honest, I still had the sneaking feeling

Wolves 3 Blackburn 0

that this wasn't really my team, and when I looked back at the booklet I had from the last time Wolves won the cup, in 1949, a match I hadn't seen, it almost meant more to me than this latest triumph, which I had. Who said football isn't a game of irrational emotions?

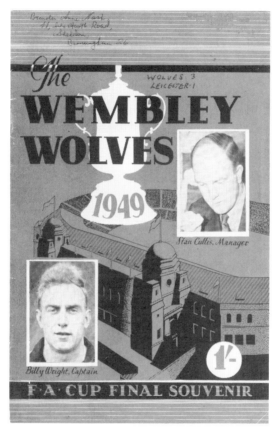

When Wolves won the cup before

However, it wasn't just my attitude to my team that was changing. Change was astir within the game itself: football was beginning to be more outward looking. There were European competitions, for a start. These days the scramble for 'places in Europe' has risen to a crescendo, with managers desperate to finish high enough in the league, or to win some domestic trophy that opens the money-spinning door to Europe for them, but then European football was considered just a distraction from the important domestic season to most managers. Matt Busby, even in the middle 1950s, had been astute enough to see that European competition was the way forward and had fought to get his team permission to enter the European Cup competition, but to most managers, Europe was a matter of some indifference. Wolves, as champions, were in the European Cup, but it wasn't taken with the utmost seriousness, and whereas nowadays defeat in a European tie would have the fans sobbing hysterically, then our lack of success in Europe was regarded with some equanimity. We beat the German side Vorwaerts in the first round, then met (with some irony, given the Munich tragedy) Red Star, of Belgrade in the second round. We beat them 3-0 at Molineux, thanks, perhaps, to the addition of a large illuminated red star (borrowed from a local cinema!) that was hung from one of the floodlight pylons. Success wasn't to last, however, and when they played Barcelona in the next round they were overwhelmed 9-2 on aggregate. It wasn't really to be until Manchester United won the cup in 1968 that the focus of attention began to shift from domestic competition to Europe, and teams really began to see such trophies as being well worth winning.

All in all, my last year before my year in France had been a good one, but my ties with the team and with football in general were becoming looser. Not only was I going to spend a whole year out of the country but, although I didn't know it then, the next decade was to change football so radically that it almost seemed to have very little connection with the game that I'd loved throughout the fifties. Football and I were never to have such an intimate relationship again.

CHAPTER 4

The Sixties

The fifties had been a decade of slow emergence from the trauma of war. Soldiers had come back from the war to a devastated country, determined to put behind them six hellish years and get back to normality and enjoyment, which generally meant football, the pub and the cinema. The years of drab austerity after the war meant that people behaved very much as they had before it, putting up with dreary, ramshackle, draughty, uncomfortable football grounds, unchanged from their pre-war squalor and queuing, not for food this time as during the war, but for the cinema on Friday and Saturday nights. The American innovations of the fifties, rock and roll, teenage liberation and Elvis Presley had awoken my generation to a new world, as yet unattainable. Even I, poor and unhappy at home, had broken away and gone to university, which opened a crack in the door of the future, through which an encouraging chink of light gleamed and I looked forward to the sixties as a time for self-improvement as well as the continuation of the glorious success story for the Wolves which the fifties had been, when I'd found on the terraces of Molineux a place to belong at last.

And, indeed, the sixties brought changes that even the most enlightened of people would never have guessed at, in all areas of our lives. Politically, it was an age of fear, of the arms race between America and Russia that culminated in the Cuban Missile Crisis of 1962, when we'd gone to bed on that fateful night in October, sériously wondering whether we'd wake up to the aftermath of a nuclear holocaust, or, indeed, if we'd wake up at all. Then came the assassination of President Kennedy in 1963 and political scandal at home with the Profumo affair and we found ourselves living in a society that was, once more, in the melting pot.

To our surprise, years of dreary austerity were followed by London's becoming the centre of fashion and style: 'youth' was in, staid, sensible middle-age was out. We abandoned our fluorescent bobby-sox in favour of long white stockings (which my mum said made us look as if we'd got dead legs). Mary Quant was the fashion guru and we all sported geometric designs in clothes, with hairstyles to match – they were sculpted and designed, rather than just cut. As for furniture, the uncut moquette three piece suites and bird's eye maple dining room furniture that my parents had taken out so much Hire Purchase debt to buy, gave way to trendy, flimsy-looking chairs with splayed-out, tubular metal legs, boomerang-shaped coffee tables made of cheap and cheerful Formica, whose spindly metal legs had on the end, not nice, solid castors, but big plastic bobbles in bright primary colours. It all looked as if it had been made by children in a craft lesson.

Fashion, and fashionable society, centred on Carnaby Street, the home of outlandish clothes and the new elite – the young – who spent their growing amount of disposable income on hedonistic pleasure. In the background lurked the 'squares', the old, the parents and other authority figures, who complained constantly about the excesses of this new society, whose eyebrow-raising antics made the front pages of the tabloid newspapers daily.

It seemed to be all change. Even that shadowy figure that skulked on street corners, or outside the local pub at weekends, trying to look inconspicuous but only succeeding in drawing attention to himself: that shifty-looking, faintly disreputable-looking fellow, the bookie's runner, who, strictly illegally, waited for punters to sidle past, pressing into his outstretch paw their bets, before he scuttled off to the office with our Dads' money to enrich his master, while we, our errand over, would trot home to await the outcome of the races and discover exactly where the housekeeping money had been lost – even he was no more, for Betting Shops became legal and Dad could go himself to the shop and watch on the TV screen where his cash had disappeared to. Progress indeed!

The Beatles came, totally changing popular music, focusing attention on Liverpool and new working-class heroes, whose culture was to dominate pop for many years. In so many areas of our lives the rise of working class culture was to have a great influence, particularly in the world of football, where the working-class hero finally came into his own.

As for myself, I had a future of my own to sort out. For one thing, I had at last begun to accept, however reluctantly, that neither of the

ambitions that had fuelled my every action during the fifties (to play
football for England and marry Billy Wright), was ever going to come
to pass. I'd begun to acknowledge the unlikelihood of the first one
when I'd been forced to start wearing glasses late on in the fifties,
which had severely limited my ability to head the ball and which
proved to be fiendishly inconvenient when playing on a muddy pitch.
To add to this I had begun seriously to suspect that when it came to
picking the England team, girls seemed to be persona non grata: they
were always overlooked in favour of men. As for my marrying Billy
Wright, that ambition had been well and truly scuppered by his
marrying in 1958, and when, in 1962, he became manager of the
hated Arsenal, I was so severely traumatised as almost to be reduced
to lying down in a darkened room and going into a severe decline. I
couldn't believe the sheer iniquity, the plain idiocy of the idea.
Arsenal! A hated London club! When the whole idea had been for
him to take over at Wolves from Stan Cullis when Cullis retired! It
was no good his saying that he'd always supported Arsenal as a boy:
it was treason, and I couldn't even think about it without feeling the
overwhelming desire to burst into tears of desolation. It was clear
that my whole attitude to football was in need of a radical overhaul.
What I didn't know was that football was coming to exactly the same
decision about itself and that the sixties was to turn out to be a
watershed in the game.

Up until the sixties, football had been the almost exclusive
preserve of the working classes: the players were working-class, the
fans were working-class, and the managers, most of whom were old
players, were also working-class. Indeed, football had a virtual
monopoly on working-class entertainment. With the arrival of the
cinema and television, however, that time-honoured monopoly was
challenged, gates began to fall and clubs began to have to look at
ways to bring the crowds back, not just the traditional working-class
spectator, but a whole new breed of fans, the middle-classes. These
sort of people, of course, wouldn't put up with the antiquated and
frequently disgusting facilities on offer in most football grounds, so
the clubs had to look at ways of updating facilities, with the express
aim of taking the game away from the traditional supporter, who was
willing to put up with anything to see his beloved team, and bringing

in the less committed who had more money. My whole happiness and identity had been inextricably bound up with the Wolves, but, increasingly, it seemed that clubs didn't want people like me, with immense loyalty but no money; what they increasingly set out to woo was a more discerning clientele with money to spend.

What the new philosophy meant first in practical terms was the updating of grounds. During the summer before the start of the 1960-61 season, Wolves carried out some work on the Molineux Street stand. In the 1950s a seat in the stand was as precious as gold dust: you had to wait for someone to die to get a season ticket to the stand – they were passed down from father to son like heirlooms. This hadn't of course, much worried the ordinary fan, for whom standing on the draughty terraces was a way of life, but the tide was beginning to turn at last, away from the grass-roots supporter to the affluent, would-be fan, who wanted comfort, warmth and shelter. Not that at this early time the philosophy permeated at all into what was going on on the pitch. The team introduced new players while I was away in France: Geoff Sidebottom took over in goal, George Showell, for so long Billy Wright's understudy at centre half, moved to full back and young Ted Farmer prepared to take over from the prolific Jimmy Murray. In fact, Farmer, this great new star whom I had never seen, scored 28 goals in only 25 games in his first season. From England came the news to my exile in France that we had scored ten goals in two matches against Arsenal, winning 5-3 at home and 5-1 away. On the face of it, and though I wasn't there to see it, it seemed to be business as usual. The team scored 103 goals that season and even managed their usual woeful cup effort, losing to Second Division Huddersfield in the third round.

Being away from the football scene, however, gave me a clearer view of the trends, and, if you had your wits about you, there were definite signs of troubled times to come. This season Wolves played in the European Cup Winners' Cup, reaching the semi-final before losing to Glasgow Rangers in a two-leg match. What made it particularly prophetic wasn't the enormous gates for the matches: 79,000 at Ibrox and 45,000 at Molineux, but the fact that, for the first time in my memory, opposing supporters caused trouble in the town centre after the match. The times, if only we knew it, were a'changing. So was the policy of players staying with Wolves for years, for personnel started to come and go. At the end of the season Geoff Sidebottom was on his way, as were Des Horne and Gerry Mannion, both of whose promise had burnt itself out in only three seasons. However, the team finished in third place in the league, even without me to spur them on to greatness and I came back from France confident of even better times to come.

....

The 1961-2 season proved to be a rude shock to the system, both to the system of football and to mine, because, in spite of my great hopes for the season, Wolves finished eighteenth in the league, their lowest position since 1933. All this mental anguish, however, paled into insignificance beside the one great change to the game that was to change the face of football for ever – the abolition of the maximum wage for players.

In 1958-9 footballers wages had risen from £20 in the season and £17 in the summer to £20 a week all year round, and many a football pundit expressed the pious hope that this heralded the end of the maximum wage. Our local football annual for the year, "The Sports Argus Annual", praised the rise in wages as being

"at least another step forward to the day when the maximum wage will be abolished and players will be paid what they are worth".

I wonder if it ever occurred to these people that the day would surely come when players would be paid what they certainly aren't worth, and if they ever envisaged exactly what a revolution such a move would bring into the game? What really happened, of course, was that with players able to earn whatever clubs would pay, the balance of power in the game irrevocably shifted, from the directors and managers, as it had been during the fifties, to the players.

After the war, the old class system that had existed before the outbreak of war, survived virtually intact. The middle-classes of the Shire Counties may well have been so shocked at the poverty and deprivation of the young evacuees they were called upon to take in from the slums of the big cities, as to support the creation of the Welfare State after the war, but the old attitudes and differences between the classes lingered on. Working class people knew their

place and expected to be ordered about and treated with
condescension by those who considered themselves to be their
betters. Certainly, footballers, even the top footballers, were treated
by the authorities at best like cretins and at worst like uncivilised
barbarians. Tommy Lawton remembered receiving a letter from the
F.A., instructing him to report for duty for an England match, which
enclosed a list of things to bring with him, which included such things
as a toothbrush, pyjamas and a change of underwear, as if he were
some deprived child going on a scout camp! Evidently the middle
class myth of the working classes using the bath to store the coal in
was still alive and well even then! Even Billy Wright, captain of
England, received terse little notes from the F.A., beginning "Dear
Wright" and offering him curt instructions: "You are to meet with the
rest of the party at the hotel ..." as if he'd been a junior conscript
receiving orders from a superior officer during the war.

Between players and Directors the gap was a vast chasm. The
Directors inhabited the Boardroom and sat in the Directors' Box,
passing any messages to the players via the manager. This, of course,
was precisely the sort of hierarchy they had been used to during the
war, and managers could quite easily be seen as the time-honoured
sergeant major, bellowing instructions and insults to his recruits in
equal measure. Players were kept rigidly in their place by
domineering managers, who stood for no nonsense and expected no
insubordination. Such an arrangement was, quite simply, expected
on both sides. The formidable Major Buckley, who ruled Wolves
from 1927-44 was one such despot, who ruled with a rod of iron. His
word was law. Stan Cullis, who came in 1948, was another such,
steeped in the virtues of hard work and the obedience to authority.
On the wall of the dressing room was a notice bearing the message,
"There is no substitute for hard work"
and it was a motto by which he lived himself and which he expected
all his players to endorse. They knew no slacking would be tolerated
and they were the fittest team in the league. Players did as they were
told, carrying on a working class tradition begun from childhood.
First they'd been disciplined at home, often with the help of Dad's
belt; then they'd been kept in line at school, any punishment given
often being reinforced by a parent when they got home, on the

principle that "You must have deserved it, or they wouldn't have given it you." Then came the forces, where unquestioning obedience was drilled into them until it became second nature. Small wonder, then, that this conditioning followed them into their work. And managers were not above humiliating players, who meekly accepted their treatment. After one match, where the winger had failed to make any impact, Harry Storer, fearsome manager of Derby in the 1950s, took the lad out onto the pitch after the match, when the spectators had gone home and walked along the touchline with him, staring at the ground. When asked what he was looking for he said, "I'm looking for the hole you fell down today."

It's difficult to imagine managers getting away with that these days, although a few vestiges of the old-time manager still remain. Brian Clough was, arguably, the last of them, for he once told Trevor Francis to take his hands out of his pockets at an Awards Ceremony and regularly told his own players to get their hair cut. Lee Chapman remembered that he also used to demand to know if they'd washed their hands when they'd been to the lavatory! He was the last of the breed, however, and his retirement severed the last link with the old days, the days I'd grown up with. What altered the relationship between managers and players, of course, was money: for the first time it wasn't the employers who called the tune, but the employees. Right from the beginning of professional football the players had been treated like serfs, bought and sold in a system that exists nowhere else but in slavery. This system had, in fact, been one of the first principles of the Football League, keen to protect the interests of the clubs (regardless of whether or not this infringed the interests of players). As early as 1897 they were looking for a system which, so they claimed, they had to have, since "unless there was more loyalty … the league would collapse."

By 'loyalty', of course, they meant forcing players to stay for long periods with the same team, preventing other clubs from enticing him away, and so putting the club which had lost a player into financial difficulties. This is why the maximum wage was introduced, to make it not worth a player's while to move clubs, since he could only be paid the same whatever club he played for. Transfer fees were introduced to compensate the club losing a player. The player himself got virtually no advantage from the move. Players were, then, simply pawns in the game of getting the league established and ensuring its financial survival.

To this end, it made financial sense not to allow players any freedom of contract, because, so the League argued, a lot of money was spent by clubs on players from an early age, money which had to be recouped by clubs when the players left them, since so few recruits actually make the grade in the game, and the money for their training has to come from somewhere. It was to be not until the 1990s that the players' view was to be considered, via the Bosman ruling.

But all this, of course, was for the future. In the early 1960s we couldn't envisage such a revolution taking place. Then came the abolition of the maximum wage, and the creation of the first £100 a week footballer – Johnny Haynes of Fulham. At once we saw the future effects of the free market, at least in embryo, for Fulham, terrified that Haynes would be enticed away to play in Italy, were obliged to dangle the carrot of wages of £100 a week before him to get him to sign for them. Actually, once he'd signed the contract, Haynes freely admitted that he'd had no intention of going to Italy: Fulham just feared he might and thus parted with the cash!

Johnny Haynes,
darling of the advertising men

Highly paid, high-profile public figures, as we all know, are of great interest to advertising men, and the creation of this new type of star soccer player brought the advertising men down to football grounds in the search for new stars. It had all started with the handsome Denis Compton, star of both football and cricket in the late 1940s, who had been promoted as the Brylcreem boy, using his charisma and dashing good looks to sell their hairdressing product. Next to be promoted was Johnny Haynes, whose face soon adorned posters and gazed at us from the windows of otherwise dreary and uninteresting barbers' shops. So was launched the advertising and media careers of a whole host of footballers in the future.

Whether or not the delicate balance of power, which had once seen managers in charge and footballers doing as they were told, changed overnight after the abolition of the maximum wage, is doubtful: at first things just went on as they had before, outwardly at least. But, coincidence or not, the next season at Wolves was one of disaster and they were never to be the same force again. Even the atmosphere on the pitch changed. In the fifties there was a great deal of humour on the pitch, both between players, and between players and referees. In one memorable match, refereed by the famous Arthur Ellis, Len Shackleton thought he'd have a bit of fun, teeing the ball at a free kick up on a little mound of peat, that had been put on the pitch before the game to stop it from becoming frost-bound, and scraped off just before the game. Twice he teed up the ball, rugby-like, on his pile of peat, only for Arthur Ellis to demolish his mini-pyramid. After this had happened three times, without a word being exchanged, Shackleton protested with a grin,
"Hey ref, there's nowt in t'rules to say I can't tee t'ball up for a free kick," to which Ellis replied, looking him in the eye and demolishing his mound yet again,
"Aye; and there's now in t'rules to say you can, either!"
whereupon they both grinned and got on with the match. In another match a player kept saying loud enough for the referee to hear, "Bad decision, bad decision," every time a decision went against his team. Then came the time when the player missed an open goal, and as he ran out of the penalty area, cursing his luck, he heard the ref saying, "Bad shot, bad shot!" Nowadays I suppose he'd get a yellow card for dissent. Once teams had to make huge amounts of money to pay their spiralling wage bills, however, and win at any cost became the rule, referees became the enemy, the one who costs them points because of his decisions, who sends off key players, gives dubious penalties and costs the team wins, points, and revenue, and so a huge wedge has been driven between officials and players, with referees being demonised and taking the blame for every defeat or every act of indiscipline on the part of the players. In our day, on the other

hand, the referee was hardly worth a mention, for we knew that over the season the luck would even itself out, for after all, football is supposed to be fun, not a war of attrition with the officials.

Actually, once the maximum wage had been abolished, it didn't take long for the true implications of the move to become apparent and for the future direction of the game to be mapped out. Astute pundits were laying out a frightening future by the middle of the decade. In the "Sports Argus Annual" for the 1964-5 season, for example, Eric Woodward made a chilling prediction that any fan of today would recognise. He claimed that the 'Super League' (which was being promoted even in those early days by some people), was already with us. He claimed that power was already concentrated in only six clubs: Arsenal, Spurs, Everton, Wolves, Liverpool and Manchester United, for he recognised that "they can outbid any of the other 86 league clubs for any promising player that becomes available". He suggested that this Super League came into being as soon as the maximum wage was abolished, and had led to a situation where "the world only wants winners, regardless of what colour shirts they wear" and bewailed the fact that "old time loyalties have been stretched wafer thin". Change the names of a couple of the super teams and we have exactly the situation that pertains in the nineties, where a few teams have a monopoly of the best players, and youngsters support the teams that are successful and high-profile rather than their local team.

I couldn't imagine that the world I'd known for so long could collapse so quickly, that the giants of my day could so soon become the minnows of the future, but the Chairman of Bolton in the 1960s, E. Garrard, saw it only too well. Only five years after the abolition of the maximum wage he was predicting exactly what would happen to the town clubs, able to compete in the 1950s with the big city clubs, but submerged in the new order:

"With the introduction of limitless wages, bonuses and signing-on fees, Bolton Wanderers soon found out that we could not compete with our wealthy city club rivals. To maintain our first division status we needed an income far greater than our population could sustain … In all, it was a poor picture for a club with the great tradition of Bolton Wanderers."

To see just how prophetic his words were to prove, one only has to look at the fate of all those town clubs, once all in the First Division and now in decline: Blackpool, Burnley, Huddersfield, Wolves, Preston, and even Blackburn (before the influx of Jack Walker's millions). These were the teams upon which the league depended in the fifties: Wolves' greatest battles were with Bolton, Blackpool, Preston and Portsmouth. Soon, all this was to be swept away.

I, like everybody else at first, didn't really appreciate quite how revolutionary the abolition of the maximum wage was going to prove, but I was soon shown in the most dramatic style, for the Wolves began a spectacular fall that was as swift as it was sudden. Just at the time when more and more income was required to pay a mounting wages bill, gates fell alarmingly, averaging only 27,000, the last game of the 1962 season drawing only 14,000 to see Chelsea. Even the local derby with West Brom only attracted 20,000 fans, the lowest gate for the fixture since 1910. Worse still, players, instead of staying with the club for years, moved with breathless rapidity and when players left or were injured, there was no-one to take their place. Both Ted Farmer and John Harris were injured and no replacements were readily available. In the past there was always a star to replace a lost one: Murray replaced Swinbourne, Deeley replaced Mullen; but now, panic-buying took over, to try to halt the decline. Chris Crowe came from Blackburn and Peter McParland came from Villa, but the decline continued, and the old and trusted players continued to haemorrhage from Molineux at an alarming rate. My old heroes, Clamp, Deeley, Mason and Stuart all left, deserting what turned out to be a sinking ship. I couldn't believe it: in the fifties everybody had wanted to play for the Wolves: now they were queuing up to leave. What, we asked ourselves had gone wrong?

Of course, when a football side hits bad times, there is no shortage of people longing to explain the phenomenon, and many people suggested that the great side of the fifties had just all grown old together and that was why the team declined. It didn't, to me, seem to be the reason at all. After all, in the past, when a player retired or was injured a young player was always waiting in the wings to fit seamlessly into the team – we'd hardly noticed the change in personnel.   Others suggested that Stan Cullis was losing his grip: everything he touched no longer turned to gold.   There may well be a germ of truth in this for the change in power structure of clubs once players could demand high salaries and call the tune at their clubs meant that managers like Cullis, who had to be the boss and were not afraid to wield the big stick if necessary, became an endangered species: their word was no longer law.   Certainly the players' attitude to Stan Cullis changed.   In his book in 1962 Ron Flowers, who had gone through all the glory years under Cullis, was saying about him, "For the good of his club he drives himself and his players to get the best possible performances out of them.   And we all appreciate him for these great qualities."

Yet, within two years he was openly attacking Cullis' managerial style and Cullis was sacked.   "Man management" had arrived, and those without   the   necessary   skills   found   themselves   surplus   to requirements.   It is certainly a situation that men like Bruce Rioch and Trevor Francis might sympathise with nowadays.

As for me, I couldn't believe what was happening.   In 1960-61 Wolves had still been a recognisable part of the old family I'd grown up with: Clamp, Deeley, Stuart, Mason, Murray, Broadbent, but by the next season the team was a bunch of strangers, a bunch, moreover, who were near the bottom of the league.   We'd managed a few wins, of course: divinity does not just disappear overnight. We'd beaten Birmingham 6-3, Bolton 5-1 and Chelsea 5-4, but we'd also been on the receiving end as well, losing 7-2 away to Blackpool and 4-0 at Everton.   We even lost in the fourth round of the cup 2-1 to West Brom, which, for the first time made me glad I was too busy preparing for my finals at university to see many matches.   I'd not been used to such purgatory and it was painful to have to suffer.   I was quite bewildered at how quickly a team who had been as familiar to me as my own family had been transformed into a collection of strangers, whose exploits on the field could no longer move me as had those of the old team.   I began to be seriously depressed when I wondered whether this was to be the end of my passion for Wolves and for football.   It seemed that everything was changed.

………

We Wolves supporters were a naive lot: we'd been used to success and couldn't comprehend the reality of failure. We'd had a fright in the last season but we never dreamt that it had just been the beginning of the end. I suppose no-one likes to admit that a loved one is in terminal decline. The fiasco of last season just had to be an aberration that the new season would put right.

To add to the problems of the Wolves, I'd got problems of my own by this time. I'd just got married and started my first job after graduation, and to the problems of my chronically mal-functioning family were added domestic concerns for my own newly-formed family, and the problems of how to hold down a new and unfamiliar job. At least, and to my relief, the Wolves offered a bit of stability this season, for they started brilliantly, beating Manchester City 8-1, then putting four past both West Ham and Blackburn. They went eleven matches unbeaten, only to lose seven times in the next nine matches, which served as a timely reminder that, just as I had exchanged life as a carefree student for the responsibilities of a husband and a job, so the Wolves had to adapt to new circumstances.

Once the early matches of the 1962-3 season were over, the winter was unrelentingly dire, with heavy snow and ice for virtually three months. To venture outside your own front door was tantamount to inviting, if not instant death, then at least a few broken limbs and shattered confidence. To go out at all meant dressing up like the now legendary Eskimo Nell and, muffled up from top to toe, you'd pass your neighbours on your unsteady progress to the shops without recognising them. Having indulged in the sadistic pastime of looking out of the window, watching passers-by going down like ninepins as they tried to negotiate the glassy pavements outside the house I decided to guard against fatal injury by wearing several layers of thick clothes, topped off by a duffel coat that resembles an ancient horse-blanket and gave me the rotund appearance of a pillar box, but which insulated me against injury, should I foolishly throw myself down a hidden kerb into the middle of the road or a freezing snow drift. Given such conditions, of course, there was no chance of any football being played. In fact, between mid-December and mid-February, more than 400 matches were either postponed or abandoned. During this time Wolves played only once, a 0-0 draw with Sheffield United, a game watched by only 10,000 spectators.

Once things got back to normal, to my relief, Wolves won 8 games out of 11 during April and May, including a 7-0 win over West Brom. When we finished fifth in the league, I breathed a huge sigh of relief, but, the rose-coloured glasses with which I'd viewed everything to do with my team in the fifties had been replaced with a hard edge of realism, which made me fearful for the future. Once they had been golden-clad gods, who could do no wrong; now they were just a once great side on the decline. For one thing, gates had fallen alarmingly: the average gate was now only 25,000, the lowest since the war, and this just at a time when the wage bill was beginning to soar. Changed from an adoring, uncritical worshipper into a realistic and worried fan, I realised that if they couldn't pay players they wouldn't get them or be able to keep them if they got them. In the fifties players would have paid to play for the Wolves: now there seemed to be no obvious attractions in playing for them. Another, bigger, club had only to beckon and our star players would be off. As if to act as an awful warning of what was to come, in the middle of the season, West Brom's international centre forward, Derek Kevan, was, quite out of the blue, and with no explanation, transferred to Chelsea, leaving the Baggies' fans stunned. So this is what the future held.

………

Being a Wolves supporter in the great days had made me entirely unused to the habit of cringing self-abasement, of going about with my tail between my legs, but the next couple of seasons were to prove my worst fears correct. My wonderful team, the scourge of the rest of the First Division, sank like a stone and were relegated to the Second Division. Sadly, the days when supporters followed their team through thick and thin were rapidly becoming a hazy, half-remembered time in the past, for, used only to success, many Wolves fans couldn't face life in the basement, and gates dropped alarmingly: anything over 20,000 was rare. To add insult to considerable injury, in the 1963-4 season we gave away, for the first time ever, more goals than we scored and home defeats were in double figures. I began gloomily to contemplate being one of those unfortunate supporters I had once so pitied, those whose club were lowly, unsuccessful and the butt of cruel jokes by supporters of more fortunate clubs. Worse still, the exodus of players continued: at the end of the season Crowe, Hinton, Finlayson, Farmer, Murray and Stobart left, and with that the stuffing seemed to go out of the team, and out of me, too. I was like an ill-used teddy bear, saggy and threadbare. In the next season, 1964-5 we won only once in the first 15 matches and relegation looked certain. The only glimmer of hope in the dark tunnel came in the form of a good cup run, for we reached the sixth round, to be beaten, (oh irony of ironies!) by Manchester United. It was scant consolation, for this was the season when Stan Cullis was sacked.

It was unthinkable – but it had happened. Cullis was a legendary figure, up there with the likes of Herbert Chapman of Arsenal, Matt Busby of Manchester United, or Arthur Rowe of Spurs. How could he be treated in this ignominious way? In the fifties the sacking of a manager was a rare occurrence, rare enough, indeed, for us all to be totally aggrieved on his behalf when in 1958 Blackpool sacked Joe Smith, the architect of all their success at the beginning of the fifties. So, when Cullis went we felt we were entering the dark ages. When we thought that in the nearly 40 years since 1927, when the famous Major Buckley took

Stan Cullis, Wolves legend

over the club, until Stan Cullis' sacking in 1964 Wolves had had only three managers, we could hardly envisage that in the next 33 years, we would have thirteen managers. This marked the beginning of the era when managers seemed to move clubs on a rota basis, like an on-going game of musical chairs.

Wolves languished in the Second Division for two seasons, coming back up to the First Division in 1967, but, as I had troubles of my own, the tribulations of the Wolves were less painful to me than they might have been. My parents' marriage had finally broken up not long after I married in 1962 and I found myself, as usual, expected to sort out the ensuing mess. I was to decide what to do with my two younger sisters, left at home with my father when my mother finally decamped for the last time, and my father, who hadn't a clue what to do with them, turned to me for assistance. The thinking was this: I was the oldest girl, so it was my responsibility. The oldest of the children, my brother, being a man, couldn't be expected to take charge: it needed a woman to be surrogate mother. Gone were my leisure days to stand on the terraces and watch football. My sisters had to be taken to see "The Sound of Music", or to the zoo, or to London for the day. It was ironic really: all my efforts to escape the stereotypical fate of the working-class girl, and now here I was, back at square one. When my first child was born in 1968, my role as mother was confirmed. If my husband wanted to spend Saturday afternoons watching football, it was only natural. If I wanted to do so it was unmaternal and neglectful of my family.

Nonetheless, and in spite of society's disapproval, we did manage to get to some matches. In October 1963 we saw Wolves, still with Ron Flowers and Peter Broadbent in the team, play out a 2-2 draw at St Andrews with Birmingham, and in the same season, a trip to London saw us watching Wolves play Fulham at Craven Cottage, and losing 4-1. We bought our Bovril at half-time from an old-fashioned refreshment bar, just as we'd done years before, and if Wolves hadn't lost, we might even have imagined that nothing had changed in the intervening years. We also saw Wolves yet again tormented by Jimmy Greaves, now playing for Spurs, scoring two goals in a 4-1 win.

I have no pride in announcing that I didn't desert my team in the Second Division, for to stand on the half-empty terraces, with all the atmosphere of a morgue, watching teams such as Bury, Rotherham and Bristol City was a doleful experience that I would not wish to dwell on. But it wasn't just the names and the quality of the opposition that had changed: everything had changed.

When I'd first become a football fan, girls on the terraces were a rare sight. Football had been a man's game, played by men, for men. And yet, although on the field things were hard, with hefty shoulder charges being the norm and goalkeepers being bundled into the net, ball and all, by burly centre forwards, clubs were always very careful that any publicity about their players should be of the very best kind, so as not to outrage traditional working-class morality and put off the fans that were their life-blood. My early scrapbooks are full of pictures of players at home with their wives, helping with the washing up, playing in the garden with their children, or sitting quietly at home indulging in blameless hobbies such as marquetry or stamp collecting. I even have a book that lists Billy Wright's hobbies as "weaving rugs and listening to classical music"! Danny Blanchflower was noted for being different, for his colourful private life that left him unwilling to be featured on "This is Your Life", but, generally, players were expected to be pillars of respectability. Gambling and drinking were acceptable, sexual adventures were not. Managers also had to follow the same code, hence the sacking in 1959 of the West Brom manager, Vic Buckingham, accused of extra-marital dabbling. It's interesting to see that today managers have to conform but players do not, as witnessed by the sacking of Tommy Docherty from Manchester United, for falling in love with the wife of a colleague, or David Pleat's sacking from Tottenham as a result of newspaper allegations about his private life.

In the 1960s came a social revolution. The miraculous 'pill' gave girls sexual freedom, Carnaby Street became the fashion centre of the world, the young all kicked their hats over the windmill and followed their instincts, however base, and predatory young women set their sights on the new super-stars – footballers. Footballers earned great sums of money, dressed in the height of fashion and thus attracted a generation of groupies of their own. The terraces filled up with girls, looking over the players with an eye to a pretty face and a pocket full of cash. The result was that footballers made the front pages of the national newspapers more often than the back pages, and more words were written about the sexual excesses of George Best than about his exploits on the field for Manchester United. He seemed to spend more time between the sheets or posing outside his smart boutiques than in playing football. Football was rapidly becoming indistinguishable from show business. These nouveau riche, working class kids, with their excesses, their essential vulgarity, were a world

Grenville Hair of Leeds
Rugmaking

Roy Little of Manchester City
doing marquetry

Manchester City's John Hart
doing crosswords

Stan Lynn of Villa,
devoted family man

Footballers 1950s style, family men and followers of blameless hobbies.

away from the ordinary, local, working-class kids who had been my heroes, men who had a sense of shame and a feeling of responsibility towards the youngsters who idolised them. Now, any kind of immorality was acceptable and, as a responsible parent myself, I felt a certain distaste for it all.

Even the football programmes were beginning to reflect the marketing of footballers as sex symbols rather than as sportsmen. In the fifties programmes had merely concentrated on statistics, results of matches, team news and the like. Now, for the first time, girls had to be catered for, and the looks of the players became at least as important as their playing ability. In 1967, for instance, the Wolves programme set aside a page in which girl supporters could vote for their best-looking player, (one girl, incidentally, nominating the young Howard Kendall!) I, who had carefully eschewed anything remotely 'girlie' in my football life, cringed.

If you want a good-looking foot-baller who is also a pleasing per-sonality then you must look at the Arsenal from whom I would choose Jon Sam-mels, Jim Furnell and Terry Neill in that order, with Jon probably the outstanding per-son.
Susan Gover, 91 Stockbreach Rd., Hatfield, Herts.

You need look no further than Howard Kendall for the best look-ing footballer. Not only that but this former Preston player, now with Everton, is also the finest wing half in The Foot-ball League. And he's a great guy, too.
Janet Shonock, 49 Walton Road, Wesham, Pres-ton, Lancs.

A handsome player, who is also a modest and nice chap is Colchester United left winger John Martin. Fel-lows like these make you wonder why so many teenagers pin up pop idols. They just don't hold a candle to profes-sional footballers.
Julie Clarke, 136 Greenstead Road, Colches-ter, Essex.

Not only is Burn-ley's Willie Mor-gan the most attractive man in the game, he is also the nicest person you could meet. He was the first professional footballer to have his own Fan Club and never did any-body deserve one more.
Judith Lawson, 3 Elizabeth Street, Padiham, Burn-ley, Lancs.

Girl power hits football!

It wasn't just the intermingling of the world of football with the worst excesses of the world of show business, and the scandalous lifestyles associated with it, however, that really did the job of alienating the old-time supporter such as myself from the game. We had a more sinister and intractable problem to confront – hooliganism. In the fifties the hooligan element of working-class youth had satisfied their urge to cause mayhem by breaking up dance halls, advertising their status by wearing their trademark teddy-boy gear: long jackets with wide lapels, drainpipe trews, heavy shoes with big crepe soles, and the greasy D.A hairstyles. By the sixties, however, with National Service a thing of the past, which took rebellious youth off the streets for two vital years, the idle youth turned their attention to football. People began to be alarmed that youngsters were getting out of control, a concern picked up by Derek Hodgson of "The Daily Express" who, in 1967, deplored the

"shouting and singing of obscenities"

at matches, blaming for this new phenomenon, youngsters under 21. This was, however, just the start of indiscipline amongst youngsters, for they soon began causing trouble at away grounds. In fact, this rising tide of unrest had its effect on me, too, for it led to my first football match sitting in the stand. I'd spent all my football life standing happily, and safely, on the terraces, but when, in April 1965, we went to St Andrews to see Birmingham play Manchester United, my husband insisted we sit in the stand. We were both keen to see the United team that boasted many of the post-war greats: Denis Law, George Best, Bobby Charlton, but, by this time United fans had begun to gain an unsavoury reputation for causing trouble at away grounds and so, choosing discretion rather than valour, we sat out of harm's way in the stand. In days gone by, I'd been at St Andrews, in crowds of more than 60,000, packed cheek by jowl next to thousands of other supporters of both teams, on the unprotected terraces, just a part of a giant sea of emotion, of a shared love for the game. Now here I was, taking refuge amongst the nobs in the stand, frightened by the supporters that had once been my friends, isolated from the grass roots that had nurtured my love for the game in the first place. It was a heart-breaking experience.

Actually, by the mid sixties, the hooligan problem was only in its infancy, but the authorities became very perturbed by it because they feared there might be trouble at the World Cup Finals, which came to England in 1966. They could not afford the world-wide adverse publicity that any trouble would create. The concern led to the newspapers exacerbating the problem by printing league tables of the worst behaved fans, among whom they singled out Liverpool and Everton supporters, who had been causing trouble back in the fifties, too. These hooligans wrecked trains and attacked opposing supporters and caused a great headache for those keen to preserve the image of the game. In fact, with the fear of hooliganism leading to a fall in gates, there were real fears for the success of the World Cup, and various plans began to be mooted, including the erection of fences. Actually, fences were not a new thing, for in 1964, when Everton had played Glasgow Rangers (whose supporters had a well deserved reputation as hooligans), there had been trouble and Everton had erected fences behind the goals, thus beginning a trend that was to change the face of football grounds all over the country in the next decade.

As far as the World Cup went, however, the fears proved groundless, perhaps because England actually won the cup. Group 'B' matches were split between Hillsborough and Villa Park, so, in July 1966, we took ourselves to Villa Park, to stand on the terraces with many thousands of other supporters and watch Spain, Argentina and West Germany. The fourth member of the group, Switzerland, played all their matches Hillsborough, so we didn't see them. What a time we had!

We renewed acquaintance with Gento, whom we'd seen playing at Molineux for Real Madrid and marvelled at the cultured play of Franz Beckenbauer, who always seemed to have plenty of time to do everything, a sure mark of a great player. We watched Germany's goalscoring centre forward, Uwe Seeler, hearing the cry of "Uwe, Uwe" from the German supporters every time their hero scored. In Argentina we saw the side that was to play England in the semi-final, the team that Alf Ramsey was to call "animals", thanks mostly, I suppose to the antics of the swarthy arch-villain, Rattin, who was to be sent off in the semi-final.

There was a real carnival atmosphere at Villa Park and we revelled in it. The stadium was alive with national flags, team colours, noises of every sort, and huge, noisy, enthusiastic crowds.

ENGLAND

22 Selected Players

1 Gordon Banks	12 Ronald Springett
2 George Cohen	13 Peter Bonetti
3 Ramon Wilson	14 James Armfield
4 Norbert Stiles	15 Gerald Byrne
5 John Charlton	16 Martin Peters
6 Robert Moore	17 Ronald Flowers
7 Alan Ball	18 Norman Hunter
8 James Greaves	19 Terence Paine
9 Robert Charlton	20 Ian Callaghan
10 Geoffrey Hurst	21 Roger Hunt
11 John Connelly	22 George Eastham

The names and numbers of the players taking part in each match will be announced over the public address system prior to the kick-off. This information should be inserted in the space provided on the relevant page for each game, covered between pages 44 and 55.

Les noms et les numéros des joueurs selectionnés seront annoncés par moyen du haut-parleur avant le coup d'envoi de chaque match. Ces renseignements sont à ajouter à la page qui convient, c'est-à-dire entre la page 44 et la page 55.

Die Namen und Nummern der Spieler welche an jedem Spiel teilnehmen, werden per Lautsprecher vor dem Anstoss bekannt gegeben. Diese Angaben können an der hierfür für jedes Spiel vorgesehenen Stelle—Seiten 44 bis 55—eingetragen werden.

Los nombres y números de los jugadores que toman parte en cada partido serán anunciados por los altavoces antes del comienzo del partido. Esta información debe ser incluida en la casilla correspondiente en la página relativa a cada partido incluida entre las páginas 44 y 55.

The squad that won the World Cup in 1966

We saw some terrific matches, with Argentina beating Spain 2-1, and drawing 0-0 with Germany, while Germany beat Spain 2-1. It was just like the old days: huge crowds, tremendous atmosphere, good-natured rivalry and the vast crush of spectators streaming out of Villa

Park after the matches, clogging up the streets outside, brimming over with exhilaration, exchanging cheerful banter with the other fans as they made their way to the bus-stop, all joined together in a shared love of the game. It was a wonderful reminder of what had once been: this was what supporting football could be; but, sadly, it was to be short-lived.

We were lulled into a false sense of security, however, by England's winning the World Cup, for when Celtic won the European Cup in 1967, to be followed by Manchester United the following year, we began to forget our fears about the English game, began to believe that it was about to enjoy a resurgence, and the optimism engendered by going to the World Cup matches encouraged even me to renew my love affair with the game. But, football as I'd once known it was like a train, pulling out of the station, disappearing down the line into the unknown distance, leaving me behind on a deserted platform.

CHAPTER 5

The Seventies

By the time the seventies came I was unrecognisable as the gawky, ill-clad, poverty-stricken kid I had been in the fifties. My parents were divorced, both married to other partners and entirely out of my life, leaving me to settle into middle-class respectability, wearing decent clothes, eating regular meals, visiting the hairdresser and being just another middle-class wife and mother of the era. I was referred to anonymously by people I met as "Peter's wife", addressed by the staff of the baby clinic as "Mother" and existed, or so it seemed, only in relation to other, more important people. So, then, nothing really had changed. All that was left to do, so it appeared, was to keep up the appearance of devoted wife and mother, changing nappies and nurturing in my breast a veritable viper, in the form of my son, who was to grow up to be a West Brom supporter, for which quaint aberration I blame entirely the pernicious influence of his father and uncle.

Indeed, the seventies was to be a bad time for all of us in one way or another. It was a decade dominated by conflict in so many areas of life. Of course the Northern Ireland conflict ground on, but we also had to contend with huge upheavals in industrial relations, which led both to a fireman's strike as well as strikes in the power industry that was to restrict industry to a three day week and reduce the rest of us, thanks to regular power cuts, to sitting in flickering candlelight, like characters in some television classic serial, like Bob Cratchit, warming his frozen fingers over his spluttering candle in Scrooge's office.

In football, to be honest, things were no better, for the seventies brought a low point in English international football. Ever since they'd won the World Cup in 1966, England had been on the decline as a world football power and, as a prelude to the relentless manager-hunting that was to haunt the eighties and nineties, people began to bay for the blood of the hero who had brought the World Cup to England for the first time – Alf Ramsey. Needless to say, he was soon out of a job and the leader of the successful Leeds side, Don Revie, the architect of Birmingham's downfall in the 1956 Cup Final, replaced him, with the task of restoring England's footballing fortunes. But it didn't quite turn out like that, for Revie, anticipating by some years the worship of money that was soon to bring the game into a pitiful state, suddenly deserted England, with two games still to go in the qualifying matches for the 1978 World Cup in Argentina, following the lure of Arabian gold to coach the team of the United Arab Emirates in Dubai, at a salary of £340,000 a year, tax free, which made the £25,000 a year he was getting for managing England look a little sick.

To make things worse, there were those who felt that it had been Revie, in his days at Leeds, who had introduced into the English game a ruthless, uncompromising sort of style, a 'win at any cost' philosophy, which, so many opined, was ruining the game. The message had certainly gone out by this time that such tactics bring results, and journalists, such as Patrick Collins of "The News of the World", was only one of the people who lamented that all they wrote down in their notebooks at the post-match interviews with managers were comments such as

"we didn't come here to entertain, we came to get a point … it was a thoroughly professional performance … we shall contest our six bookings … we play it hard but fair."

In an attempt to counteract this sterile philosophy, the League introduced the system of three points for a win instead of two, to discourage teams from playing for a draw away from home, but the 'points before entertainment' philosophy had taken hold.

Perhaps it was hardly surprising, with all the conflict about us and the huge changes that were coming over football that the seventies was the first decade when I didn't see a single live match. I followed the game exclusively through television, watching "Match of the Day" with all the avid interest I had once lavished on "Sports Report" on the radio, when Eamonn Andrews had brought me the word of God. Of course, I wasn't the only football fan who stayed at home, safe behind my own front door, for the seventies, that age of conflict, belonged to the hooligan.

There had been little organised hooliganism in the fifties, but, as the sociologists tell us (and they, we are assured, know about these things), football had, since the mid-fifties been undergoing a process of bourgeoisification, which meant that, in order to attract a wider and richer clientele into the game and combat falling gates, clubs made a determined effort to bring in the middle-classes with their new money. We'd seen the efforts in the sixties, where new toilet and catering facilities had been introduced, a small gesture aimed at attracting more discerning and sophisticated people into football grounds. By the seventies, with revenue more and more desperately needed, this process accelerated, leaving the poor, traditional, working-class fan, to whom their team was their life, unwanted and unappreciated.

What had first set off the process, really, was the big slum-clearance programme in the East End of London in the sixties. In 1968 we began to see in the East End groups of young men gathering, who were to become the scourge of football throughout the seventies. The Skinheads, (a name that was soon to be feared in football grounds throughout the country), were as recognisable in their uniform as the Teddy Boys had been in theirs in the 1950s. The Skinheads wore, not a parody of Edwardian dress, long jackets, velvet collars and the like, as the Teddy Boys had done, but an obvious parody of traditional working-class labourer's dress: big, heavy working boots, jeans cut off before the ankle to show the socks and emphasise the size of the boots, large and conspicuous braces holding up the trousers, shirts with button-down collars and the trademark cropped hair, advertising their origins as sons of toil.

At the beginning it was easy for me, brought up in deprivation on a Council estate in a big city, to have sympathy for them, for they were definitely the abandoned and dispossessed of society. Their slum estates in the East End, places of close communities and shared loyalties, had been bulldozed and replaced by monstrous high-rise concrete blocks where hundreds of strangers lived cheek by jowl like battery hens. Houses were sold to outsiders, to immigrants and middle-class people, looking for somewhere cheaper to live, and all community meeting places were destroyed, leaving people with no roots and seemingly no shared history. They didn't feel they belonged any more to the places that had belonged to them for generations. All that remained, for the most part, were the old football grounds, which had grown up in the very areas from which they drew their support. To the skinheads, these were oases in a desert of destruction, the only places that still gave them a feeling of belonging. I, who spent years relishing a feeling of belonging at Molineux, could understand their feelings only too well. My association with a football team had given me a sense of identity and I could easily appreciate their need for an identity that was being ruthlessly destroyed. You only have to look at aerial photos of Upton Park to see how it is an island in a sea of faceless, alien tower-blocks, devoid of all sense of community.

Upton Park – an oasis in a desert of redevelopment

Because the mere sight of the skinheads was so intimidating and alien, middle-class people liked to present them, even in the early days, as merely yobs looking for trouble, who knew absolutely nothing about football. Yet they were wrong, at least at the beginning, for these rootless, half-educated kids, often of low intelligence and with no background, had only one thing in their lives, only one thing they knew anything about – football. They were almost all extremely knowledgeable about their team, its history, its successes and failures, and they clung to it because it gave them a history and something to be proud of and to share in. Unfortunately, their methods of supporting their teams often included the confrontational and aggressive style which is so typical of working-class life. They guarded their team, protected it from insult and injury, defended their territory on the terraces, captured enemy territory if possible and were top dogs in their own ground. Ironically, of course, the more fervent and therefore aggressive they became in defence of their team, the more of an embarrassment they became to their clubs, who then wanted to be rid of them. Thus they found themselves outsiders again, rejected again, belonging nowhere.

What the skinheads were rebelling against at first was the clubs' desperate attempt to take football away from the working-classes, to get a new, clean, civilised image that denied the past and rejected the very people who had made the game successful in the first place. Horrified by these uncivilised yobs, who wore their club colours like war-paint and echoed the conflict on the pitch in conflict on the terraces, clubs did all they could to sever these unsuitable links with the past, even to the extent of changing the clubs' colours, colours as old as the teams themselves. The old colours, often 100 years old, were often just simple contrasts. If there were two teams in a town, one had red, the other blue: Liverpool/Everton, Manchester United/City, Sheffield United/Wednesday, which focused crudely on the physical conflict that was so much part of working-class life. People needed something, some cause, to fight for (even metaphorically). Indeed, this conflict was carried further in many cities, where the two clubs represented a crude religious divide: Glasgow Celtic/Rangers, Liverpool/Everton, Manchester City /United. To many people this deliberate changing of club colours seemed a rejection of all that football had once stood for, intrinsic conflict and tribal loyalty. It was, so many people felt, a conscious attempt to take the conflict out of football, wipe out the passion from the game, to sanitize it to make it more palatable to the more squeamish middle-classes.

An integral part of football's appeal had lain in the need to stand together on the terraces, in close proximity to other like-minded people, for it filled a vital role in working-class philosophy. Football was like boxing for the working-classes, in that it provided conflict and physical confrontation, a test of physical prowess, yet bounded by clearly set out rules. Both sports offered a trial between hard men, who could both dish out punishment and take it: a legitimisation of a certain amount of rigidly regulated violence, whereby winners and losers could easily be recognised. Whenever England played Ireland in Tommy Lawton's days as England's centre forward, he always sent the Irish goalkeeper, Elisha Scott, a bottle of aspirins before an England-Ireland match with a note:

"Take all of these. You'll need all the sleep you can get before the match!"

and would then spend the whole ninety minutes trying to bulldoze him, ball and all, into the back of the net, while Scott made every effort to flatten him as often as possible. It was, in those days, all part of the game. The motto was, "It's a man's game". What was more, the link between spectator and player was made stronger by the fact that the players were the same sort of people as the fans: they'd had physically hard lives, they knew the threat of debt and the dole, they knew the lives and ways of the spectators intimately. That's why football had such a seemingly eternal grip upon the emotions of so many people.

By the seventies, however, this was no longer the case. The players were highly-paid superstars, aping the middle-classes in dress and lifestyle, cut off from the poor fans, in their mock-tudor mansions in the country or in the leafy suburbs. As these superstars demanded higher and higher wages to support their new lifestyles, so clubs had to come up with more and more schemes to raise the revenue their teams could produce. This, of course, left the old-style supporter more and more on the outside.

Nothing illustrates this divide between traditional support and the new image of football than the rush in the seventies for clubs to build new and luxurious (not to mention fiendishly expensive) stands, with bar and social club facilities, for use, of course, only by the rich, who

could afford season tickets to these palatial stands.   It was all reminiscent of the Nicolas Bentley rhyme:
"Happy are the rich
Who can afford the clubs
Where they can go on drinking
When the poor have left the pubs".
In 1978 Wolves planned such a stand, a 9,000 capacity, all-seater stand, with 42 executive boxes and splendid bar facilities, to entertain this new breed of supporter, whose money was to be the saviour of the game. What it turned out to be, in fact, was the beginning of the end for Wolves, for it was not opened until 1982, had cost £2 million to build, and, with the team relegated to the Second Division, they found themselves with a debt of £1,988,000.

The same thing happened to other clubs, of course, eager to take their image up-market. The experience of Chelsea, for example, mirrored the Wolves' unhappy experience. From 1963 to 1972 Chelsea had experienced enormous success under managers Tommy Docherty and Dave Sexton and grand plans were formulated for a luxurious new stand, the largest yet built on a British ground, with 11,500 seats and costing £1.6 million. Unfortunately, while it was still under construction, first came the industrial unrest that led to the three day week, which delayed building, then the average gate fell by 23%, then the team was relegated, all of which served to push the club into near bankruptcy. Finally, the stand was finished a year late, in 1974, the cost had risen to £2 million and by 1976 Chelsea were in debt by £3.4 million.

But worse was to come. The attempt to bring the game up-market, the posh new facilities only invited the scorn of the grass-roots supporters. To the skinheads it was the team that mattered:
"What's the use of have a f...ing palace for a ground when we haven't got a team?"
was their judgment.   And, indeed all the efforts at making stadia comfortable and middle-class merely fuelled violence amongst the spectators who saw it all as a means of driving them out. A palpable rift grew up between clubs and their erstwhile fans, and the fans reacted to their growing feelings of frustration with violence, which soured relations between them and their clubs even more.   The

spectators wanted the money spent on the team; the clubs, desperate
to increase revenue, wanted it spent on the grounds, to attract more
spectators, and the predictable result was violence. At Wolves during
the decade, attempts by the local press to help alleviate the hooligan
problem by arranging a meeting between the fans and the club,
ended, predictably, in stalemate, for the fans wanted money to
strengthen the team and the club, faced with average gates of only
23,000, wanted to spend the money on the ground, to attract more
revenue. They intended in install more seating, to discourage
violence and encourage middle-class supporters, but these plans
merely fanned the flames of hooliganism in old supporters and
exacerbated the problem of violence. In the last match of the 1975-6
season, Wolves had to beat Liverpool at home to stand any chance of
avoiding relegation. Not only did Liverpool win the match, before a
crowd of 49,000, but their supporters, hooligans of long pedigree, laid
the town of Wolverhampton waste, before leaving a trail of
destruction all the way back home up the M6.

It seemed just to be a vicious circle. The more hooliganism there
was at grounds, the more gates fell; the more gates fell, the more
desperate clubs became to solve the problem by installing more
seating and better facilities. This led to the old-style fans, seeing
themselves rejected, to indulge in more and more violence. Indeed,
what I and, I suppose, most people remember of the seventies is the
violence, the terrifying, casual maiming and even killing of innocent
people and the climate of fear that this engendered, not only in
football fans but in the population at large. Once word got round that
good sport could be had, beating up people at football, every violent
psychopath joined in, and no-one was safe. Once we'd worn our club
colours with pride: now it could get you maimed for life by opposing
supporters. So afraid did we become that we wouldn't let the next
generation of supporters, our children, go to matches for fear that we
wouldn't see them again. It was ironic really: in the fifties my dad
had been afraid to let me go to football, when there was absolutely
nothing to fear, and twenty years on, here was I, really afraid, and
with reason, for the safety of my own child. Actually, the threat was
real enough, for the original aim of the skinheads of intimidating the
opposition's fans by 'taking their end' had escalated into terrifying

violence, which, as time went on, was characterised by increasingly sophisticated strategies to avoid detection. For example, West Ham's efficiently organised hooligan squad, the self-styled "Inter-City Firm" (ICF), travelled, as their name suggests, not by football special but by ordinary Inter-City trains, which enabled them to avoid detection and thus surprise 'the enemy'. Their names showed that they saw themselves as businesses, businesses whose product was, so they seemed to suggest, "mayhem". This new brand of hooligan went incognito: no club colours, nothing to suggest any connection with football at all. They were anonymous, unremarkable young men in suits, to the casual observer just young businessmen going about their business, which made them all the more frightening and deadly. They carried weapons: knives, CS gas and petrol bombs, and, as time went on, people were actually killed in their attacks. The West Ham group actually adopted the chilling practice of leaving their business-cards on victims, reading

"Congratulations: you have just met the ICF."

As the decade wore on, and hooliganism became a way of life, extremist groups such as the National Front, playing upon the skinheads' dislike of immigrants, who had moved into their traditional home areas, began to recruit members on the terraces, and so hooliganism took a new turn – a racist one. When hooligans attacked and broke up shopping centres they singled out for attack Asian shopkeepers, and, before too long, this overt racism, encouraged by the National Front, spilled over onto the football field, with black footballers being singled out for abuse.

The predictable result of what seemed to be Chicago-like violence on the streets of Britain, where shopping centres became no-go areas on Saturday afternoons and people who lived near grounds stayed indoors and waited for their windows to be broken and their cars to be vandalised, was that the new generation, the children, were kept away from matches and people began to question the future of the game. The Ibrox disaster, where 66 people died, only served to remind people that football meant trouble and was rapidly becoming a social evil.

With everybody's attention riveted on what was happening off the pitch, it was hard to concentrate on what was happening on it, which was a pity, really, because there was much to entertain. There wasn't much at Molineux to inspire, that's true, for the Wolves continued to decline, slipping into the Second Division in 1976, though they came back up the following season. What we did have was a myriad of new cup competitions, dreamed up to try to increase revenue for the clubs. Wolves played in the League Cup, the Texaco Cup, the EUFA Cup, the Watney Cup. They reached the semi-final of both the FA Cup (which saw, for the last time at Molineux a crowd of 50,000, for the game against Coventry), and they lost in the semi-final of the League Cup, which they won the following season, beating a Manchester City side, which boasted as its forward line, Mike Summerbee, Colin Bell, Francis Lee, Denis Law and Rodney Marsh!

Another on-going entertainment of the seventies was watching the outlandish fashions sported by the players. This was the age of the ludicrous flared trousers that flapped round the ankles like a runaway newspaper in the wind, wide kipper ties, reminiscent of the wide-boy Arthur English, and huge mops of hair, accompanied by untamed sideburns, which had many of the players looking like werewolves. Seeing a picture of Charlie George, long lank locks and all, in a news-paper, induced my young daughter to assume he was our next door neighbour's sister, so, for ever more since he's been known to us as "Dean's mother"! All in all, never have footballers been a more risible bunch. On the pitch the decade belonged to Liverpool and Kenny Dalglish who, to my chagrin, was not born an Englishman. They won the league 5 times in ten years, and the European Cup twice. Then Brian Clough's Nottingham Forest won the European Cup and we could almost imagine we were back in the old days: no violence and tough, dominating managers. Clough seemed to get out of players, by his old fashioned managerial style, what even they didn't know they had. He transformed a team of honest triers into a world-beating side and when players, whose market price had rocketed as a result of their success with Forest, went elsewhere, no-one else had the magic to bring out what Clough had seen in them, as Garry Birtles and Peter Davenport, seduced by the lure of Manchester United, were to find out.

The seventies, outside football, was a time of shrinking job opportunities and unemployment, yet, within the game, players, as

well as looking quite laughable off the field, were earning small
fortunes on it, but never did the supporters think of begrudging them
their vast earnings. The poor, the unemployed, the disadvantaged all
seemed to take a vicarious pride in seeing these working-class lads
made good and enjoyed the spectacle of them joining the middle-
classes, sending their children to private schools, joining golf clubs
and mixing with the nobs on equal terms. To the fans the players
were still the same as them and, since traditionally, the only ways for
the poor to make money were in crime, boxing or football, they took
great pleasure in seeing how many working-class lads made it into
wealth via football. Even the press, so it seemed, accepted the
trappings of affluence enjoyed by the top players with a remarkable
degree of equanimity. Patrick Collins of "The News of the World",
for example, writing of England captain Bobby Moore, declared that
"he is, in my view, more than welcome to his £35,000 house, his
Daimler, his businesses and his good living".

On the field, however, the huge wages, which led to the urge to
win at all costs changed the game for the worse, for the same Patrick
Collins decried the fact that even ten year olds were expected to play
a 4-4-2 system and aped on the field the petulance and rough play
they saw in the professional game,
"screaming at referees and faking anguished injury at the merest hint
of a tackle".
However, all the mumbo-jumbo about various systems of play was
put into humorous perspective by a Hull City programme, when it
reported asking a spectator:
"What does 4-3-3 mean to you?"
only to get a puzzled look, followed by the tentative answer,
"Ten?"

However, rough play, win at any cost, began to be linked in the
minds of those whose job it was to stamp out hooliganism with
trouble on the terraces, the premise being that the one inflamed the
other. Of course, rough play was nothing new in the game. After all,
my father had refused to turn professional in the thirties because the
league was so rough that he feared serious injury, and Billy Wright
well remembered the days when every team had its hard man, its
'chopper', who revenged during the course of a match any injuries or

slights, real or imaginary, suffered by his less formidable team-mates. Billy Wright told the cautionary tale of a young winger whose career was ruined by one of these self-style avengers, who, made to look foolish as the boy winger sped past him time and again, finally despatched him off the pitch and onto the cinder track, which kept him off the field for good. Compared to this, so Billy Wright thought, the modern game was gentle in comparison. Brian Clough's reaction to foul play was typically hard-edged:

"If you're still conscious and yer leg's not broken, gerrup and gerron with it."

Nevertheless, rough play was beginning to be a problem that was exercising the authorities, already at their wit's end to solve the seemingly intractable problem of hooliganism.

The problem of how to stop supporters from maiming and killing each other within grounds was to be solved, so we were told, by erecting fences within the terraces, to keep rival fans apart, fences all round the pitch being envisaged to stop pitch invasions and rival fans rushing to the other end of the ground to get at their enemies, the opposing supporters. We'd all seen pictures, of course, of grounds in South America, with deep moats to prevent the fans from storming the pitch and lynching the referee, but the thought of such things happening here appalled us. After all, we were not over-excitable Latins, like the Brazilians who had buried the ball in the sacred Wembley turf, once, when incensed by a refereeing decision. But the authorities were adamant: we needed to be fenced in, and soon an increasing number of football grounds took on the appearance of zoos, with spectators confined to metal cages, where they clawed at the bars and tried to reach opposing supporters, who tapped on the bars and teased them, like a naughty child teasing a monkey at the zoo. What a sad and frightening spectacle it made, to see thousands of people behind metal fences, like the inmates of a concentration camp, treated like wild beasts, confined in cheerless metal pens. For the first time in history, football fans were not welcomed into grounds, not treated as visitors or patrons, but were grudgingly accepted into places with high walls, and empty, sterile zones, which gave them the feeling of being prisoners. They were feared and controlled in a hostile way, processed like cattle, often kept back for hours after the match until the home supporters had dispersed, in an attempt to prevent trouble spilling over into the streets. Gone was all pretence of making football grounds friendly, opulent, comfortable places of leisure, forgotten was the goal of attracting a new clientele to the game. In its place we saw the process of trying to exclude undesirables, on the premise that once the troublemakers were eliminated, new people would be attracted to the game.

As for me, it sent a chill down my spine. Just after the war I'd been taken to Sutton Park, on the outskirts of Birmingham, to see an internment camp, holding Italian prisoners of war. It was a cheerless place, with spartan huts, hemmed in by barbed wire and the faces of the poor, dispirited men incarcerated there haunted me for years. They were not the horned and cloven-hooved monsters we'd been led to believe our enemies were, and I remember saying, with the disappointment of a seven year old,

"But they're only men!"

So were the football fans I saw penned in, imprisoned just because they wanted to watch a football match. What had happened, I wondered to the good-humour, the sheer fun that football had once been to its devotees. Why had Liverpool become an exporter of mayhem, when its citizens had the wit, in the days of Ian St John, in the 1960s, to add to a poster outside a church, which asked the challenging question:

"What shall we do when the Lord comes?"

the perfect rejoinder:

"Move St John to inside right!"

I couldn't believe that the sharp wit that gets a bus-driver in Liverpool to answer the question,

"Is this bus going to Speke?"

with the instant, deadpan answer,

"Well, I've been driving it all day and it hasn't said a word yet!"

could just disappear. Common-sense, decency and humour had to re-assert themselves sometime. But while we waited for them to do so, we skulked behind our closed front doors and gave football a miss.

CHAPTER 6

The Eighties

In the innocent days of the fifties we hadn't really thought about football at all in any seriousness. Yes, of course, we agonised for days about whether our star player would be fit enough to play on Saturday, worried about whether or not we'd win a game against our fiercest rivals, and contemplated sadly a drop down the table when we'd lost two matches in a row, but we never gave the slightest thought to the future of the game. As far as we were concerned, football was as timeless and as immutable as the Almighty himself. Yet, thirty years later, not only did football come to be seen as not eternal at all, but questions began to be seriously asked about whether the game had any future at all, whether keeping football was worth all the loss, the sacrifice and the tears. Just when, with my children growing up, I was contemplating following the game from the terraces again, suddenly it became a moot question whether there was going to be any football for anyone to follow.

If the seventies had been the age of the hooligan, the eighties, at least for most of the decade, belonged to the bailiffs and the Receivers.

The first inkling of the turmoil and confusion that was to fill up the whole decade came in the salutary story of the Wolves who, during the course of the decade, were to come within three minutes of ceasing to exist at all. During the first years of the eighties they slipped down the league with all the rapidity of sliding down a greasy pole, finally ending in the basement, the Fourth Division. A friend of mine, a Swansea supporter, took comfort, when his team were in the Fourth Division, from the fact that they couldn't fall any lower. I, however, just couldn't believe what had happened to my team. I wasn't much mollified by the fact that by the end of the decade they had managed to claw their way back to the dizzy heights of the Second Division, for the nightmare just seemed to go on and on. Personnel changed at the club so rapidly that it was more like Clapham Junction in the rush hour than a football club. Managers, players, owners, all came and went so lightning fast that you didn't even have time to learn their names. There were seven managers, a whole host of players, but the chief interest, and easily the most vital, centred on the owners of the club.

The decade began badly, for in the 1980-81 season the team finished in 18th place in the league, and by the next season they were playing to rapidly falling gates of no more than 11,000 and, worse still, they kept losing matches. To add to the troubles, the supporters, always vocal and demanding, were putting increasing pressure on both team and manager and demonstrations were becoming a regular part of matches at Molineux. Not surprisingly, no manager was very keen to take the job and when Alex Ferguson wisely declined the offer it was Ian Grieves who accepted the poisoned chalice and the end of the season saw the club £2.6 million in debt. Thus followed the first big scare of the decade, for the Receivers were called in and the summer was filled with horrifying rumours of the club's imminent demise.

This was the atmosphere that greeted the players when they returned for the 1982-3 season. Just as the winding-up order was due to take effect (three minutes before, actually), up popped Derek Dougan, a most unlikely good fairy, to save the day. This last-ditch effort, however, was only the cue for the pantomime to continue, with a mass exodus of personnel that was to continue for the next few years. Back came John Ireland, the former chairman of the club, to be the President, and, to everybody's surprise and delight, the team gained promotion at the first time of asking.

If we all breathed a huge sigh of relief at this, however, it was to prove premature, for the traumas of the previous two years had unnerved everybody and gates fell dramatically, with only a measly 6,000 watching home matches. With no big stars who could be sold to raise money, the team again sank into the Second Division. There was so little money in the kitty that the players didn't know from one week to the next whether or not they would be paid, and as morale plummeted, so did the team. Player after player was drafted in to try to halt the slide: you hardly got time to learn his name before he was off again, so it really wasn't a great surprise when the team sank all the way to the bottom, to the Fourth Division. I could hardly believe what was happening.

The blame for the spectacular decline was laid at the door of the mysterious backers, the Bhatti brothers, who had, so we thought, funded Derek Dougan's takeover of the club. They were shadowy figures, who were hardly ever seen, and who seemed sometimes to exist only in myth, a situation that led Tommy Docherty, who had been engaged to save the sinking ship, to comment with some exasperation,

"How can you work for people you don't see? Howard Hughes and Martin Boorman could be found more easily than the people who own Wolves."

What was worse, it seemed that these secret benefactors didn't have the sort of money they'd claimed to have when they'd first taken over the club in 1982. It was the bitterest of ironies that when the Bhattis had bought the club, a rival bid by millionaire Sir Jack Hayward had been turned down in favour of them. How much heartache would have been saved for their long-suffering supporters had Sir Jack just upped his bid a little and thus secured the club in 1982?

But history tells us that he didn't, and we had the painful spectacle of Molineux, so ramshackle by this time that only two sides of the ground could be opened for safety reasons, being home to the disaffected and angry on the terraces and the bewildered and barely competent on it. And yet, in spite of those of us who remembered the glory days being heartbroken by the painful spectacle of the great shrine to excellent football becoming no more than a junk heap, against all the odds, the club pulled through and by the end of the decade they were in the Second Division and had won one of the myriad of new cup competitions, the Sherpa Van Trophy, (which some wag said sounded more like a Dutch striker than a trophy!), in 1988. All that was required now was to cling on by their fingertips until 1990, when they were taken over by Sir Jack Hayward and we could at last contemplate the club's lasting into the next century.

Of course, Wolves were not the only club that suffered the hand-wringing horrors we had just gone through. The eighties was the time of near extinction for many clubs. Tranmere Rovers were saved thanks to financial help from Wirral Borough Council and Birmingham City's see saw battles for control of the club almost exactly mirrored those of the Wolves. Burnley, who came perilously close to slipping out of the league altogether, which would certainly have meant extinction for the old club, won the last match of the season, thus avoiding relegation, and the highly emotional scenes that greeted the win, and a certain reprieve, with fans crying openly and embracing each other, bore witness to the deleterious effect of such stress on the poor supporters of the Cinderella sides. Many clubs during the eighties continued to exist only thanks to a sympathetic bank manager and many supporters found it depressing to go back to the decaying old stadia, scenes of former triumphs, and find them reduced to heaps of neglected junk.

It was this sort of backroom wrangling, with clubs changing hands regularly, bought by anyone willing to put money in, this hand-to-mouth existence that so many clubs were forced to live, that drove a final wedge between clubs and their former supporters, who had spent so long standing on ramshackle terraces, to watch mediocre and ever-changing teams, without any hope that money would be found to repair either. This, of course, was simply another spur to the hooliganism that had blighted the seventies. Even as late as 1989 Graham Taylor was enumerating the frustrations of being a football supporter thus:

"The glory days of regular big crowds have gone forever. Fans see clubs spending millions, while they are expected to pay £1 for a programme. They see executive boxes installed while they are peeing down one another's legs in scruffy, inadequate toilets. They read about huge sponsorship deals, while they are drinking stewed tea and paying more for a piece of stale cake than they paid last year."

Graham Taylor had, in fact, put his finger squarely on the problem. It was not that money was not coming into the game – it was – it was just that no-one saw any necessity to spend any of the vast sums coming in on the grass-roots supporters. More and more the fans had it made plain to them how little they mattered. Enormous amounts of money were beginning to go on transfer fees for players. During the fifties, the highest fees in the English league rose from only £35,000 to the £45,000 that Manchester United paid for Albert Quixall in 1958, (though, incidentally, a pointer to the future could be seen in that in 1957 Juventas paid Leeds £65,000 for John Charles). The sixties saw transfer fees of over £100,000, while these had doubled by the seventies. During the eighties, thanks largely to the inflationary prices paid by Italian and Spanish clubs for British players, for example £1.5 million for Ray Wilkins by AC Milan, and £1 million by Barcelona for Steve Archibald, by the end of the decade fees of more than £3 million were commonplace. All this rapid inflation had been fuelled at the end of the seventies by Chris Waddle's transfer from Spurs to Marseille for £4.2 million, and from then on, the sky was to be the limit. This naturally led to the chief interest of clubs being to raise more and more revenue, which left the poor supporters out in the cold once again.

All this turmoil, the money that came into clubs and never filtered down to the supporters led to a continuation of the hooliganism that had so blighted the seventies, and the rise of other manifestations of anti-social behaviour, including the racial abuse of black players. In the rougher, yet more innocent, days of the forties and fifties, nationality was just another term of insult to throw at a person, along with his wearing glasses, or being fat, or bald. It had no great social significance. "You great Irish git" was no better or worse than "Old foureyes" or "Baldy". It was just an insult, and race was never an issue in itself. Actually, in the fifties there were very few black players: Bill Perry of Blackpool and Charlie Williams of Doncaster are just two who come to mind. They were likely to be abused for things they did, or did not do on the field, but not just because they were black. By the eighties, however, with more and more black players coming into the game, it began to be a real issue. By this time the National Front had done their worst, recruiting into their midst many football fans, many of them the Skinheads that had caused football such grief in the seventies, and black players were regularly insulted and humiliated from the terraces every match. Bananas were thrown on the pitch, monkey noises and gestures were made every time a black player touched the ball, and some clubs were even noted for not employing black players at all. It thus became an embarrassment for many civilised fans to have to listen to such abuse and to watch black players having to endure such humiliating treatment. It didn't, of course, matter to the yobs that many of the players they so mercilessly abused were some of the most talented players of the age: John Barnes and Viv Anderson, for example. They suffered, just the same.

This unsavoury situation was just another nail in the coffin of football support and clubs had to turn their attention to raising revenue from other means than just gate money, in order to cover both greatly increased transfer fees and spiralling player's wage bills. Thus, they turned their attention to television, which was to take the running of the game almost out of the hands of the football authorities and into the grateful hands of the television companies. For the proverbial mess of potage; £25,000 for each of the 92 league clubs, the League agreed to change the habits of a lifetime of many fans, by agreeing to have some matches staged on Friday evenings, or Sunday afternoons. By the end of the decade, this blood money, which ignored the spectators' wishes, was increased to £200,000 for each club, which ensured that the clock would never be put back to the days of football on a Saturday afternoon, and that the wishes of the fans would count for even less.

With the frantic scramble for clubs to raise more money degenerating into something of a bun-fight, it wasn't surprising to find all manner of weird and wonderful schemes cooked up to keep teams afloat. A plan to have Fulham and Chelsea share a ground, either Stamford Bridge or Craven Cottage, was superseded by one for Fulham to merge with QPR, call themselves Fulham Park Rangers and play at Loftus Road! This plan was finally abandoned, but with all that was going on both on and off the pitch, with matches being played on days and times suitable to the television companies, the wonder was that anybody managed to watch any football at all.

Actually, the televising of matches, allied with the clubs' desperate need to raise yet more revenue, was to have another effect on the game, perhaps unexpected. Clubs went into merchandising in a big way, stocking club shops with replica team strips, bags, scarves, hats, in fact anything you could put a club logo on, and this, allied to the huge national publicity given to the top clubs, via television coverage, began to change the pattern of football support, which had been virtually unchanged since the turn of the century, when fathers passed down their allegiance to a team to their sons. Many youngsters, forbidden by fearful parents from watching live football in the hooligan-plagued seventies, had been brought up almost exclusively on television matches, watching the big teams that, before the advent of television coverage, had only been names to them, and they deserted their local teams in favour of these more glamorous teams they saw on television every week. Thus in Walsall you began to see youngsters wearing the strip of Leeds or Manchester United, carrying their books to school in bags that advertised Arsenal or Tottenham Hotspur, and support for less glamorous local teams began to ebb away. In the fifties people generally supported their local team, there were no proofs of allegiance save the woolly scarf and the knitted bobble-hat and a rosette for Cup ties; now clubs were competing to sell anything and everything to an insatiable public who, presumably, sat in front of their television on Saturday night, clad in their team strip, drinking their tea out of a mug bearing their club name and colours, scarf round their neck, hat perched foolishly on their head, cheering with a fervour that we once reserved for the terraces on a Saturday afternoon, a team they'd never actually seen play in the flesh.

It's easy, of course, to laugh at these armchair supporters, who never see their teams play, but it is nevertheless true that the eighties weren't really a time for real, live football supporters, for, within a space of five years we had three major disasters that reduced far too many live supporters to dead victims. The turbulent past caught up with the game at last.

First came the Bradford fire disaster in 1985, which killed 56 people and seemed to be a tragic proof of just how little supporters had come to matter. Once, football disasters had been reported dispassionately, by an unemotional newsreader, which distanced us from the horror, but this time horrified television viewers saw the disaster as it unfolded. First there was the agonising sight of panic-stricken supporters fleeing the flames, desperately trying to reach the pitch to avoid the fire, while behind them, the old wooden stand burned, immolating 56 fans and injuring many more. A pile of rubbish, carelessly left under the wooden stand had ignited, the stand had gone up like tinder, and people had died.

Then, we had scarcely had time to recover from the trauma of this experience before, no more than a fortnight later, came Heysal, where mindless mayhem led so-called football fans to ignore the game and fight to the death with people whose only crime was that they supported a different team, violence which left 39 families mourning a loved one, and proved to us that hooliganism had taken a new and more deadly turn. Not content with causing fear and chaos at home, the hooligans had exported it to the Continent, and English football fans soon gained a deserved reputation for being the most violent in Europe, which Heysal proved so graphically. At this shock, witnessed by so many people who'd never been to a football match in their lives and had no real idea of the carnage that could be wrought in the name of the game, people began to ask seriously whether we needed football at all: after all, they argued, it was just a game, and no life was worth losing just for game. The subject was endlessly chewed over in the media, with no real consensus on just what was to be done to cure the sickness. Then, just as the subject was beginning to die down in the public consciousness, came Hillsborough, when yet more innocent people were sacrificed to football's inability to put its house in order, for, indirectly, the Hillsborough dead were victims of the hooligan problem that had already been with us for nearly twenty years, killed by the barriers put up in the decade before to fence in the violent and the anti-social.

Hillsborough was to be a watershed in the game, a disaster too far, a tragedy which reverberates still, for a line has yet to be drawn under it: how can it be forgotten when vital questions such as why and how and whose fault it was have yet to receive satisfactory answers?

All we remember is the sight of blind panic, of young children laid lifeless on the pitch as bedlam raged about them. We didn't even have the emotion-deadening effect of body-bags, anonymous and clinical, to screen the victims from our view and sanitise the whole tragedy. These were real people, really dead, and all for wanting to watch a football match. Trying to fence people off, to keep them from each other had backfired spectacularly, and people had died, totally unnecessarily, so it is hardly surprising that the whole future of the game should be called into question. After all, it was the bitterest irony that in the middle of the eighties, Highbury, which had used to be a Semi-Final venue, had removed its fences, only for a pitch invasion to take place by Everton supporters. Frightened by this, the authorities gave Arsenal an ultimatum – put the fences back or lose your status as a Cup Semi-Final venue. That Arsenal refused to reinstate fences meant that Hillsborough was named because Highbury was no longer in the running to stage the match.

In spite of the tragedies of the era, however, we didn't entirely lose sight of the football itself, for to watch the greatest exponents of the art is always a pleasure, and in the eighties there was still Liverpool. They had dominated the seventies, with powerpacked Kevin Keegan, small, industrious and deadly given a sight of goal, and that most formidable of defenders, Tommy Smith, he of the face resembling a wanted poster in a children's comic, of whom Bill Shankly once said, "he could cause a riot in a cemetery".

The eighties brought us the eccentric Bruce Grobbelaar in goal, straight out of the tradition of eccentric goalkeepers begun by Charlton's Sam Bartram, who was known to head the ball out of the penalty area long before it became an essential skill in the goal-keeper's armoury. Grobbelaar was a man whose dress sense was as outlandish as his goalkeeping style. One minute he'd be flinging himself spectacularly across the goal to make breathtaking saves, the next he'd be charging recklessly downfield, like a forward member of Custer's cavalry. Then we had Ian Rush; slight, unremarkable even, until, that is, he got a sight of goal. He could turn on the proverbial sixpence and rifle the ball into the net before a defender had registered that the ball was at his feet.

Then, of course, we had Manchester United, led by Captain Marvel, Bryan Robson, who dominated games by sheer energy and commitment, backed up by the formidable Norman Whiteside, who ploughed through defences with all the finesse of a tank. Seeing him brought to mind another, earlier, Norman, Norman Hunter of Leeds, who wasn't called 'bite your legs' for nothing. We even had a "Boys Own Paper" hero in Gary Lineker, who scored goals like clockwork, and never bit or savaged anyone. He was idolised by a whole generation of youngsters before, in the nineties, his mantle was taken over by the veritable "Roy of the Rovers", Alan Shearer.

In spite of all that was good on the pitch, however, and heroes are thrown up in every generation for our delight, all was not well with football. Hooliganism was still a problem, and the headlong pursuit of money was threatening to make clubs forget the fans altogether. In an effort to combat hooliganism and bring back families to football,

some clubs tried the experiment of having family enclosures, with an all-inclusive price for parents and children. They enrolled youngsters into junior branches of the club, offering them birthday goodies and meetings with the players as incentives to join. Unfortunately, such laudable attempts to bring football back into the realms of civilisation were all too often doomed to failure, with family enclosures vandalised by hooligans and youngsters terrified and intimidated. Perhaps the best epitaph to such a praiseworthy failure was pronounced by Trevor Hicks, who lost both his daughters at Hillsborough:
"Football is the one thing we did as a family. Now we're not a family any more."

So, sadly, the abiding memory of the eighties was tragedy, for the decade was dominated by Hillsborough which, along with the Taylor Report that followed it, was to have the most profound effect on the game in the next decade. Soon, control of large crowds, the design of football stadia and, indeed, the future of the game itself was to be occupying us all once again and many of us began to wonder where the heart and soul of the game had gone. Hooliganism had cost clubs huge amounts of money, with English clubs being banned from European competition for 5 years after the Heysel affair and yet, in spite of the damage such evil behaviour had brought to our national reputation there were still many voices clamouring to have English clubs reinstated, even though no real progress had yet been made to make sure that English yobs couldn't engineer another Heysel. Fortunately, there was a more sane voice on this issue, John Smith, Chairman of Liverpool and the Sports Council, who said,
"There is no way that English clubs should be allowed back yet. It is too soon. There must be a longer penance. More importantly, our public is not psychologically ready. We need a longer period out of European competition to break the habit of people travelling abroad for violent purposes. We cannot inflict havoc on our fellow communities in Europe in the name of football. No game is worth that. We alone export hooliganism, and I am disturbed that one or two influential people in English football are pressing for the ban to be lifted".
These were words that were to come back to haunt us in the next decade, the nineties.

CHAPTER 7

The Nineties

The forty years since I began supporting football in the 1950s have brought so many changes that sometimes I wonder if it's the same game at all. The only constant in an ever-changing world seems to me to be the fact that everybody in the game is still as entirely crazy as they were all those years ago. Take the Chairmen of football clubs, for example. They are persuaded to pour millions of pounds into a football club whose chances of prosperity are slight to say the least and whose commercial viability would have any self-respecting accountant waking up in the night in a cold sweat, only to find that if the new expensive ground and even more expensive players fail to work the desired miracle, these now impoverished benefactors will look out of their windows one morning to find a demonstration outside their house, with fans bearing placards with the ungrateful legend "Chairman Out!", leaving them to come to terms as best they can with their overnight transformation from fairy godmother to the wicked witch of the North.

As for managers, their role has changed so much over the years that it's hard to credit that anybody but a lunatic would take on such an eminently thankless task. In the 50s managers were vague, shadowy figures, ignored by the media and supporters alike, left to get on with what they did (and we weren't all that clear what they did do), free from intrusion and criticism. It wasn't until the 60s and 70s, when player power really began to bite, that managers acquired a new and unenviable role – that of universal whipping-boy. With the crazy logic that you only find in football it was believed that, although it was the players who really determined what went on on the pitch, or even the Directors who allowed or forbade transfers, who were to blame when a team was not successful, the scapegoat for such failings would inevitably be the manager. His certain dismissal as soon as results began to go against his team and fans began uttering rumbles of dissatisfaction was always the safety valve that let the guilty off the hook and offered the fans some small sop to their hurt feelings, while reassuring them that the Board were taking the club's lowly position seriously. Still, in spite of the innate unfairness of it all, managers still continued to accept their role as Aunt Sallys and to move from club to club in an ongoing game of musical chairs.

Now, however, the manager business has taken on a new, more sinister turn. A new way to humiliate managers has been found. Of course, it may be that a manager is to blame for buying a player who turns out to be a flop, but now Chairmen have taken it upon themselves to buy or sell players without even bothering to inform the manager about what is going on. What remains to be seen, however, is whether the Chairmen who humiliate managers such as Walter Smith and Harry Rednapp will succumb to the age-old panacea for all football ills by sacking their manager should the team be unable to struggle on without the star player that the Chairman has sold.

As further proof, if proof is needed, that everyone in football is inherently barmy, we have only to look at the players. Not only do they earn a living playing what is essentially a kids' game – hence the unedifying sight of players behaving like eight year olds, grabbing the ball to take a throw-in, fighting the opposition player who comes to get it, even though they know they put the ball into touch; pushing and jostling any other player as they wait for a free kick to be taken, just like kids shoving each other in the playground; moaning at the ref just like kids saying "please, sir, he's pushed me!"; or rolling about the floor like silly kids, shoving and tapping at each other when a goal has been scored. And yet, although they're just overgrown kids playing a kids' game they seem to believe in a touchingly naive way that not only is what they do of immense importance but also that they ought to be paid inordinate amounts of money for doing it.

As for the supporters, they also just have to be mad, for the nineties have called upon them to endure the worst treatment that any age has yet forced upon them.

What has scuppered the fans in the nineties has been yet another shift of power within the game, comparable to the enormous upheaval caused by the scrapping of the maximum wage for players in the 1960s. In fact, it's been an age of all change. With regard to the Wolves, most of the change has been for the better, for the dire trials and tribulations that beset them in the eighties have been replaced, thanks to Sir Jack Hayward, with real hope for the future, even if the promised land of promotion is still a mirage, seen but not reached, notwithstanding the efforts of Steve Bull, the latest in the line of great Wolves centre forwards. Nevertheless, with a completely rebuilt Molinuex and new hope, the club has finally risen from the ashes of the awful eighties.

The old and the new Molineux

As for football itself, it seems that even the game has gone crazy in the nineties. It's stopped being a game, a simple matter of twenty two men kicking a ball, watched by partisan and appreciative spectators, and has become so much a part of high finance that it takes an accountant to follow it at all. There's no doubt about it: in the nineties the game belongs to the money men. With clubs floating on the Stock Market, becoming PLCs with shareholders to satisfy, football had ceased to be a sport and has become just another business, like making screws, cars or cardboard boxes. The future of the game is no longer in the hands of people with the game's best interests at heart; the managers, football authorities, spectators, but in the hands of the backstage men in suits, the money-men, who dictate policy both on and off the pitch. Indeed, it seems more and more that what goes on on the pitch on a Saturday afternoon (or rather at whatever time on whatever day the television companies decree that the matches will take place), has very little to do with the real business of the clubs, which is now, like most businesses, to make a profit and offer handsome dividends to their shareholders.

With this in mind, it didn't take a great deal of foresight to see that the teams who see themselves as the elite of the game would do everything to distance themselves from the rest of the 92 clubs in the league, market themselves as a superior product, raise money just for themselves and jettison the poor relations. It was, then, no real surprise when in 1992 the Premier League was created, by the breaking away of the top clubs of the old First Division. The aim, of course, had nothing to do with the promotion of football as a sport in the country, and everything to do with enriching themselves by any means possible, to enable them to pay the spiralling costs of transfer fees and players' wages necessary to stay at the top. The first way they chose to do this was via television money. The very first television deal with football had offered the same modest sum (£25,000) to all the ninety two league clubs, to help the smaller clubs stay afloat. Now, the Premier clubs negotiate their own deals with the highest bidder, leaving the lower clubs to shift for themselves and go into decline and, in some cases, liquidation. Of course, not everybody in the game thinks this is a good idea: some people fear that the demise of the lower clubs will mean the drying up of talent, from which the big clubs sought their stars. David Pleat, for example, commented:

"I'm worried. The corner shop is going out of business. The breeding grounds could disappear if we don't act soon."

What David Pleat didn't appreciate is that the big clubs don't need home-grown talent any more. A fat cheque book can buy you all the stars you need from abroad. Once we never saw foreign players, except in international matches, now we see them every week, making up the bulk of some of our domestic sides. Watching Chelsea is now like watching a crack continental side, such as we used to see under the floodlights at Molineux all those years ago. They have the same silky skills, every player so easy and comfortable on the ball that it's a pleasure to watch them, all flair and expertise. And yet, they are a foreign side, masquerading as an English league team. What made English football unique is being squeezed out in favour of a continent-wide product, which is the same from England to Russia, which ignores national skills and aptitudes in favour of a homogenised product that can be sold world-wide.

Of course, today's fans, brought up with this internationalism will see it as all very natural. They will think it normal that their team is so packed with foreign players that there's now nothing to differentiate football in England from that in Spain, or Italy, or France. They won't mind, perhaps, that the rich clubs of Europe, the Juventus', the Barcelonas, the AC Milans of the world, sign every good player of whatever nationality as soon as he becomes available, for fear that some rival might get him, only for many of their expensive signings to move on at the end of the season, in a constant stream of comings and goings, as still more players are brought in, in the frantic search for the ideal permutation. Hence, in the Italian league, the substitutes are often world-known names, who drift in and out of a team over a season, who are changed so often that you often can only tell what team you're watching by the colour of their shirts. The players, hardly knowing who they'll be playing for next season, and desperate to shine when they get a game in the first team are sometimes so afraid of failing that the football they produce is safe, sterile and boring.

Whatever we didn't have in the fifties we did have stability and the lack of stability is the one thing that marks out football very clearly in the nineties. It is, predictably, one of the things that people of my generation bewail most often, and which puts us off the game now. Nat Lofthouse deplored the fact that all the money in the game has meant that

"the style's gone and so has the loyalty".

Is it really only us old-timers who long for a team we can relate to, players we can support and get to know over a period of years, a group consisting of managers, players and fans who all pull together for the good of the club? Now, the situation of the old days where players stayed with clubs for years has gone for ever. Players now are simply mercenaries who will play for the one who will pay the most.

Of course, this is not surprising, since footballers have become a part of showbusiness, employing, like showbiz stars, agents, who will negotiate the best financial deal for their clients, devising contracts that will allow their clients to desert a club after one year if they do not get what they think they are owed, a place in Europe, the Premiership Trophy or the FA Cup. They are merely hired at enormous cost, while insisting on their get-out clauses, which will enable them to leave after a year with never a backward glance, with scarcely a hint of gratitude to the fans who have supported them, worshipped them, made them into heroes, bought shirts bearing their name and cheered them on, week in, week out. Players have become spoilt children, whom nobody dares upset, lest they take their skills to your rival. Fans are beginning to complain that players, who earn more in a week than most fans earn in several years, can hardly be bothered to play for their teams nowadays, so wrapped up are they in their pop-star girlfriends, modelling contracts and showbiz lifestyles. Offering value for money to the long-suffering fans seems, for some players, to have become a very low priority. Indeed, we have reached the point where, so many players, paid vast amounts of money, and a good deal more than the managers who are supposed to control them, feel they can do as they like. George Gavin, in "The Birmingham Evening Mail", told the story of a famous player who asked his manager how much he would be fined if he missed training for a couple of days. On being told, "£2,000", the player calmly took out his cheque book, wrote out a cheque for the required sum,

and handed it to his bemused manager with the words:
"See you in a couple of days."
Even at international level, sadly, the same attitude seems to prevail,
for when, recently, the German national team had a run of mediocre
results, the manager, Berti Vogts, explained it thus:
"What to you expect? I call up eleven players and I get eleven
millionaires. What do they care?"
Whatever happened to power bringing responsibility, I wonder?

What I find so amazing in this situation is that with the growth of
players' earnings, the poor, the deprived, the unemployed fans who
keep them in business don't seem to resent these vast earnings, any
more than the fans envied Johnny Haynes' £100 a week in the 1960s.
There are beginning to be rumblings that players aren't worth the
money they get, but fans are still willing for an old player, past his
best, to go to a lower club and earn £17,000 a week, (more than they
earn in a year), and if one of these prima-donnas should threaten to
leave a club because they refuse to pay him what he's most certainly
not worth, there are always supporters who will tell the club, via the
local newspapers,
"Give him the money. He's a good lad".
It certainly bemuses the old-time managers and players, for Tommy
Docherty once commented:
"I played with the legendary Tom Finney – he earned £14 a week.
Today we have players who are on £8,000 a week for sitting on the
subs' bench and can't even play properly."

Actually, it is this point that is most disturbing about modern-day
players. We never now see players moving from the Premiership to
the First Division (unless they're old and over the hill). Such is the
climate of sloth in young players that it seems that many of them are
quite content to pick up several thousand pounds a week for playing
in the reserves of a Premiership team, rather than try for first-team
football (and perhaps a reduced wage) in a lower division. It doesn't
auger well that our youngsters are willing to settle for what Milton
once called "Ignoble ease" rather than try to better themselves.
Perhaps Karren Brady, Managing Director of Birmingham City was
right when she claimed that in her experience footballers are
"only interested in drinking, clothes and the size of their willies".

What has more and more put me off football, however, is the growing feeling that more and more the fans count for less and less. The business of football clubs is now making money and the football fan merits scant attention in that system. Bill Shankly, who knew something about football, once averred that
"A football club is a marriage of the team and the supporters," but, sadly, that is no longer the case. The scramble for money has driven a wedge between the fans and the players and some clubs even seem to be quite content to do without supporters to watch the team, as long as they spend their quota of cash in the club shop.

Actually, there are other aspects of the modern game that have served to discourage the ordinary, working-class fan, that blindly devoted supporter such as I used to be in the fifties, supporters who find fulfilment in following their team through thick and thin. The first nail in the coffin of this old-fashioned type of supporter came as a legacy of the Taylor Report after Hillsborough, a report which insisted upon all-seater stadia as an attempt to make football grounds safer for spectators. It was all done with the best of intentions, of course, but it took away from the old grass-roots supporter his age-old right to stand on the terraces, with thousands like himself, a solid phalanx of adoring fans, worshipping at the shrine of their beloved team. In the fifties it had been the players who were treated like serfs, ordered about and patronised by their self-appointed betters: in the nineties this unenviable position now belongs to the fans. The message has gone out: poor, working-class people are no longer wanted, and barriers have been erected to keep them out. Clubs now are not interested in the poor supporter who buys a ticket each week out of his pay or his dole money. What they want are the vast sums of money that can be generated by corporate hospitality suites for big business to entertain important clients and thus to keep the wheels of industry turning. Under the influence of the money men, Newcastle supporters are only welcome if they buy a season ticket: the few pounds it costs to buy a single ticket is scorned, for there's always enough people to fill St James' Park, without having to rely on the poor. Thousands of fans can't get into Old Trafford each week, but the club can find room for representatives of local businesses to entertain their clients in an endless round of corporate business hospitality. My son, a West Brom supporter, was invited by a client to be his guest at Old Trafford, where he saw a match, had drinks with the players afterwards and had his photo taken with the League Cup (which United held at the time). What would an ordinary Manchester United fan have given for that experience! And yet, ordinary fans can't even get a ticket to the ground. I never thought I'd ever see the day when fans were so shabbily treated. It all smacks of the bad habits of the nobby events such as Wimbledon, when the plebs are forced to watch the proceedings on the television while in the marquees at the All England Club, rich businessmen, invited to the club as a spur to business deals, ignore their tickets for the Centre Court and sit in the marquee eating their strawberries and cream and throwing the odd, uninterested glance at the action on the television.

To add yet more humiliation to the humble football supporter, Manchester United put up notices warning that anyone who stood up would be ejected from the ground and they have since turned their attention that the other undesirable working-class habit – singing at matches. As a final patronising gesture to their already insulted enough fans they have graciously announced that they may keep a small section of the ground where singing will be permitted. Thus, the bourgeoisification of the game, begun in the late fifties, is nearly complete and the poor, disadvantaged supporters have finally been swept away from the grounds that, once upon a time, they felt they owned.

As if to emphasise that the grass-roots spectator, the poor fans in the backstreets who made football what it was, is no longer wanted, and that football as I once knew it is dead, many clubs, shut in in inner city locations where they can't expand are moving grounds, away from the traditional areas of support to the leafy suburbs of the outskirts of towns, well served by motorways. Since the 1980s, thanks to grants to help implement the recommendations of the Taylor Report, there has been a rush to re-locate, begun by Scunthorpe in 1988, who moved out to the edge of the town. They have since been followed by clubs such as Walsall, Huddersfield, Middlesbrough, Sunderland, Derby, Stoke, Chester, Bolton. Of course, it may be that new facilities were long overdue, but so many clubs, on moving, have cast off their roots by giving these fine new stadia new names.

'Roker Park', 'Burnden Park' and 'the Baseball Ground' are dead, and in their place have come up-market names such as 'Pride Park', 'the Stadium of Light' or names that show nothing but naked commercialism, such as "The Reebok Stadium'.

The old: Wrexham

The new: Huddersfield's McAlpine Stadium

In order to bury the past even deeper, and raise even more money from the shamefully exploited supporters, teams have now abandoned their old colours, a process begun in the seventies to try to discourage hooliganism. It is now reaching the heights of commercialism, for teams now have to have official away strips, which they wear regardless of whether their main colours clash with the opposition's. Home and away strips are changed every year and away strips have no connection whatever with the traditional colours of the club. Indeed, some clubs, such as Manchester United, find it convenient to put out anything up to six different strips during the same season, because their cynical money-men know that crazy, fanatical United fans will fork out for them all and keep the tills ringing merrily. Nowadays, it's often difficult to recognise which team's yours when they run out onto the pitch, when you're wearing last year's green and yellow away strip and they are now clad in this year's red and yellow, chocolate brown or even black.

What do the money-men care that there still exists in supporters a deep longing for tradition, for an affirmation of their roots? An old Bolton fan, having just watched his team beat the mighty Liverpool in the cup, commented with some satisfaction,
"It's nice to see t'lads playing in white socks again,"
and when Jack Walker took over Blackburn, he insisted on a return to the traditional blue and white halved shirts which, to him and to so many other fans, were synonymous with the team and which represented as much as anything Blackburn Rovers FC. Is it just old-timers, old fogies trying to resurrect a dead past or is it people who understand what football support is all about, trying to re-discover the soul of the game?

In my worst moments I fear that there's precious little of the soul to save, for now it isn't the management of clubs who decide who will be hired or fired, but the money-men, trying to maximise profits. The fact that players are only too willing to desert clubs at the drop of a hat may well be fuelled by their impression (in essence true), that they are looked on by clubs as being nothing more than merchandise, a commodity that can be sold on the open market, like coffee or toilet rolls, at the whim of an employer, regardless of the player's view of the matter. If it makes financial sense to sell Andy Cole from Newcastle to Manchester United, what do the money-men care that a devoted fan, (somewhat overwrought, to be sure!) has, only the week before, had a large picture of his hero tattooed on his leg! Who cares if Kevin Keegan has to be sacked in order to keep the price of the club's shares stable? Now, to add to all this, we have the Bosman ruling, which has given rise to the unedifying spectacle of clubs desperately trying to off-load players who might fetch a good price, before their contract is up and they can go without a fee. What price the fan's voice being heard here?

Like other football fans, I wonder where it will end. If money is to be the only god, not the game itself, then football as I once knew it, is dead. Financially, of course, 92 clubs are totally unviable: even a First Division, left to pick up crumbs from the Premiership table, is doomed to decline. Premiership clubs, scared silly by the spectre of relegation and the decline that this inevitably means, will ultimately vote out the clubs at the bottom, the clubs that see-saw between relegation from the Premier and promotion from the First, leaving an elite group of about a dozen clubs, into which all the wealth and talent of the game are concentrated, insulated from the threat of relegation, playing each other several times a season to fulfil enough fixtures. These teams will then find themselves playing to a handful of spectators, while the millions who have been forced to subscribe to the satellite television channels in order to see football at all, will sit at home and watch it on television. It is a vision of hell.

As I see it, the one glimmer of hope for the game seems to be that although the money-men of the game might be able to decide when and where a game is played, what colours the team play in and which players play for a team, they can't change fans, the people who all have the same needs as I had when I first came to be a football fan all those years ago. These people, pushed out of the places where they once felt they belonged are at last beginning to make their voice heard and beginning to band together to make people listen to their demands for the right to have a voice in deciding what happens to their teams. Even as early as 1967 a warning note had been sounded, when the Spurs' Secretary, RS Jones had warned:
"Spurs will create more seats as the demand grows, but even in London, many fans prefer standing accommodation. They say they get a better atmosphere."

The more clubs try to marginalise or ignore fans, the more they will feel this basic need for the solidarity of thousands of like-minded people, bound together on the terraces, all with a shared aim, a shared passion.

There may, of course, be no going back, but it seems to me that when the self-styled experts tell us football fans what we want they might just be making an almighty mistake. After all, football had as its basis, almost as its raison d'être, all those years ago, rivalry and conflict, the more local the better and so when fans are offered a European Super League, featuring English teams that haven't even had to win a domestic trophy to get there, with teams being invited to join on the basis of whether they are considered a 'big' club or not, might they not prefer a league filled with today's first and second division teams, Port Vale v Stoke to Liverpool v Barcelona? After all, how many fans can go regularly to Europe to watch their team play top foreign sides, and how many fans would soon get tired of Bayern Munich v Juventus, teams in which they have no real interest at all? What the innovators forget is that for most people it is passion that fuels football, and most English fans would prefer Liverpool v Manchester United any day to Liverpool v Benfica.

With this in mind, it is by no means foolish to suggest that a European Super League might mark the return of armchair supporters to the grounds of the lesser clubs, to experience first-hand again the passion of supporting a real, live team. After all, supporters might be bossed around, told what they should want, and ignored by the rulers of the game but they can vote with their feet, leave the "Euro-football", with its homogenised, un-English product and get back to the grass-roots. How will the television moguls cope then, televising big European matches which take place in empty stadia – no noise, no singing, no atmosphere. Perhaps the fan will have the last laugh after all. Once, teams wanted our fanatical support and reacted to it with kindness, appreciation and gratitude. I wonder if it's too late for that to happen again?

POSTSCRIPT

In September 1996 I went back to Molineux to see the recently erected statue of Billy Wright, outside the stand that bears his name. I have to admit a lump came to my throat as I looked up at it: it was him to the life. It had the same characteristic turn of the head, the same expression as he ran out onto the pitch before a match. The memories came flooding back, and, seeing his name on the stand in large letters, and the John Ireland Stand, and the Stan Cullis Stand, I was back again, all those years ago, waiting for the players to come out of the dingy entrance, past small, grubby, 1930s windows, which gave the place the look of a factory, and into the car-park for me to get their autographs. The ground is totally different now, of course, a vision in gold, all-seater, with a luxurious entrance foyer, deep-piled carpets and comfy sofas, a huge portrait of Billy Wright dominating one wall, for all the world like the reception area of a prosperous city company. But, seeing the names I knew so well, it still seemed like home.

As I stood there, looking at the statue, seeing ghosts, letting the nostalgia wash over me, a coach pulled up outside the entrance and disgorged the current team, returned from a training session. Had such a thing happened to me forty years ago, I'd have been in paradise, surrounded by all my heroes, scurrying about, trying to get all their autographs before they disappeared inside, trying to catch a word with my favourites, autograph book clutched in my hot little hand, trembling with emotion as I looked at all the real, live heroes. But, as I eyed them curiously, trying to think of all their names, it struck me suddenly that far from the golden heroes of my youth, they just looked like a group of unremarkable, faintly scruffy kids. As I slip into respectable, matronly, late middle age, I wonder ... can I be growing up at last?

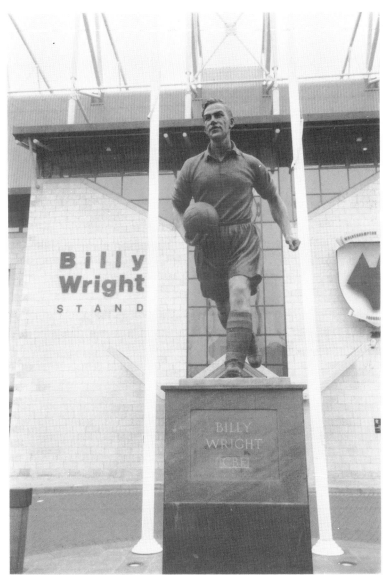

Billy Wright's statue outside the new Molineux